THE BIBLE
IN 40 DAYS

THE BIBLE
IN 40 DAYS

Discover God's plan for your life

**CHRISTIAN ART
PUBLISHERS**

Published in South Africa by
CHRISTIAN ART PUBLISHERS
PO Box 1599, Vereeniging, 1930

© 2007
First edition 2007

Cover designed by Christian Art Publishers

Unless otherwise indicated Scripture quotations
are taken from the *Holy Bible* New International
Version®. NIV® Copyright © 1973, 1978,
1984 by International Bible Society.
Used by permission of Zondervan
Publishing House. All rights reserved.

Scripture quotations marked NLT are taken from
the Holy Bible, New Living Translation, first edition,
copyright © 1996. Used by permission of Tyndale
House Publishers, Inc., Carol Stream, Illinois 60188.
All rights reserved.

Set in 11 on 14 pt Palatino LT Std by
Christian Art Publishers

Printed in China

ISBN 978-1-86920-798-4

07 08 09 10 11 12 13 14 15 16 – 11 10 9 8 7 6 5 4 3 2

Contents

INTRODUCTION

It sometimes seems as if men are given greater preference in the Bible. They are depicted as leaders, kings, and are usually also the heroes.

However, their shoulders have to be strong as a great deal is expected of them. They have the responsibility of caring for their families and being good fathers to their children. They have to make important decisions, carry many responsibilities, and serve the Lord faithfully.

Moreover, they have to be an example to others, as Paul said to Titus, "Teach the older men to be temperate, worthy of respect, self-controlled and sound in faith, in love and in endurance" (Titus 2:2). It seems as if God had a great deal of trust when He created men because the paths of men and God run close together.

This book tells about the journey that God and people take together. Of course there are highs and lows along the road ... yet through it all we learn a great deal about God's grace and love. We learn that when we fall God is gracious and merciful. He will help us up to continue on our journey. We learn all about the joy and peace of being truly human as we walk with God along our life's path.

The message of each book of the Bible has been summarized for you, helping you to grasp the essence of the Bible in a nutshell. Because each section is so concise, you will be able to get a good overview of the message of the Bible. You can read the whole Bible in a short time.

In the second part of this book we discuss some of the most important lessons that we can learn from the Bible in 40 days. We will learn more about God and His Spirit that is at work in us, how to live a meaningful life, where to draw strength from in tough times, and other important life lessons.

Why 40 days? Well, 40 is the number that symbolizes the world as a whole in the Bible. For this reason you will get an overview of the entire biblical message as God intended it.

Once you have finished with this book it will open up a whole new depth and meaning for you when you read your Bible. You will know why the Bible is such a wonderful light on every man's path.

THE STORY OF
THE BIBLE

– In a Nutshell –

The Bible is a library of books (66 books in total) that tells us a great story … the story of God and people. Here's a brief account of what we can expect from the books of the Bible:

THE BIBLE TELLS US ABOUT THE HISTORY OF GOD AND HIS PEOPLE. WE READ ABOUT THIS HISTORY IN MANY OF THE BOOKS IN THE BIBLE.	
GENESIS	God made all things, but people turned their backs on God. So, God called Abraham and his family to be His own people. They were sent to Canaan. The story of Abraham and his children, Isaac and Jacob, is vividly told with wonderful imagery. Through love, sadness and corruption, this family eventually landed up in Egypt where Joseph, Jacob's son, was appointed as second in charge to the king. This was a very important position.

EXODUS	Jacob's descendants stayed on in Egypt, but they were treated so badly by the Egyptians that God eventually freed them. He sent Moses to save them. God then took them on a journey to the land He had promised them.
	They had to cross a desert to reach the Promised Land. It didn't always go that well, yet God promised them that He would always remain their God if they would faithfully serve Him. So God gave them the Law at Mount Sinai as a sign of this agreement (covenant) between them.
LEVITICUS AND NUMBERS	God gave His chosen people rules to organize their lives so that they could be socially, spiritually and physically healthy. The new nation then moved as far as the banks of the Jordan River. Just on the other side lay the land that God had promised to them.
DEUTERONOMY	At that point God's people needed to prepare themselves before they could enter into the Promised Land.
	Under Joshua's leadership they eventually entered into the Promised Land. It was not easy. They had to fight for every inch of the land they claimed, but God faithfully helped them.
JOSHUA	Eventually the whole land was theirs, and they divided it among themselves. More tough times still lay ahead.

With the death of Joshua they were without a leader in Canaan and they simply did what they wanted. There was little sign of obedience or order. God saw their struggle and so He raised up leaders (judges or magistrates) whose task was to help the people through these difficult times.

During this very stormy period the people began to look up to Samuel who was a highly regarded religious leader (a bit like a prophet or a priest).

Samuel was the one who appointed the first king of the nation. His name was Saul. Saul started out well, but that didn't last long. He soon became corrupt. In the meantime David, another great leader, emerged in the background. David eventually took over the reins from Saul.

It was not easy going for David, but in the end the struggle was worth it. The nation was united under one king. David established Jerusalem as the capital city, and consolidated the kingdom of the Israelites. This heralded the start of a golden era. Sadly though, sin overcame David, and his life was eventually tarnished by disobedience.

David's son, Solomon, succeeded him. He was a very devout man, and became widely known for his great wisdom. He ruled with great skill and even managed to fulfill his father's dream of building a temple for the

Lord. When he disappeared from the scene it was not long before the history of the nation took a turn for the worse.

One king quickly followed another. Many of these kings were poor rulers. As a result, the kingdom was split in two (the northern kingdom – that consisted of 10 tribes – and the southern kingdom, or Judah, that consisted of the tribes of Judah and Benjamin).

The nation did not serve God as they should have, so God punished them for their disobedience; they were defeated in war by the Persians and the Babylonians and were taken out of the Promised Land as slaves. They had to live in exile in foreign countries.

Eventually they were allowed to return to their own land and their beloved Jerusalem. Upon their return they set about the task of rebuilding the temple that had been torn down. Again, these were difficult times, but the Jews persevered!

Ezra re-instituted the Law as the book of rules for the nation and prepared everything so that the nation could worship God again, as they longed for, in the temple.

Nehemiah was the one who rebuilt the walls of the city of Jerusalem and ensured that the people knew exactly what to do in order to serve the Lord in faithfulness and righteousness.

The next 400 years of the history of the nation of Israel can be read in the apocryphal books. Alexander the Great conquered all of the nations in the East, even Israel.

The nation was ruled by the Greeks for many years until the Maccabees (a Jewish family that could no longer stand Greek rule) helped the Jews fight their way to freedom.

However, this didn't last very long. They were soon under the yoke of Roman rule as Rome took over the world.

Jesus was born under Roman rule in the town of Bethlehem. We don't know much about His childhood, but in the Gospels we are introduced to Him as the Messenger of the Good News of God. He proved that He was sent by God through the many miracles and wonders He performed.

The religious leaders of the time didn't approve of Jesus. His message of God's new world, a world that is being drawn back to God in love and faithfulness, threatened their religion. So, they got rid of Him by crucifying Him.

However, after three days He rose from the dead and appeared to His disciples!

They were overwhelmed by this miraculous event and immediately believed that God had sent Him. No one could keep them quiet! The Good News of Christ had to be told throughout the whole world.

The message first spread through Jerusalem, and then to nearby Samaria … When the floodgates opened there was nothing that could stop the spreading of the Good News. The waves touched the farthest reaches of the world, it was heard even in the very center of Rome.

Apostles such as Philip, Peter and especially Paul, proclaimed the Good News throughout the world as it was known at that stage in history.

They told everyone about the Lord; from small groups of women that gathered by the rivers to serve the Lord, to prisoners in jail cells, on ships, and even in the palaces of kings. They proclaimed Him who seeks people out and makes them His beloved children.

God's promises and faithfulness to His people enabled them to live secure within His mighty hand.

They looked forward to a time where God Himself would live among them. Wherever He was, there they would be. He would dry away their tears and give them hope and a future filled with joy and peace.

"Come, Lord Jesus," is the very last prayer in the Bible.

THERE ARE ALSO BOOKS IN THE BIBLE THAT GIVE US HISTORICAL INSIGHTS INTO THE LIVES OF REMARKABLE WOMEN.	
RUTH AND ESTHER	There are some women in the Bible who influenced the history of Israel in important and remarkable ways. Ruth was not even an Israelite, but through her faithfulness she became a great-grandmother in Jesus' own lineage. Esther saved the nation of Israel from certain catastrophe by her brave deeds.
THEN THERE ARE BOOKS IN THE BIBLE THAT TELL US HOW WE CAN FILL OUR ORDINARY LIVES WITH GREATER MEANING. THESE BOOKS OFFER US TIMELESS WISDOM.	
PROVERBS, ECCLESIASTES AND JAMES	How do you know when you're playing the game of life as God wants you to? What is it that makes life truly worth living? How should a person live in order to have a meaningful life? You get answers to these questions, and many more, in the books that deal with wisdom.
JOB	What do you do when life has dealt you some painful blows? Does suffering mean that God doesn't love you anymore?
SONG OF SONGS	There are many blessings in life, such as the love between a man and a woman. These things are meant to be enjoyed, in fact you can sing joyful songs about them!

PSALMS	Talking about singing, one of the books in the Bible contains 150 songs that cover just about every topic in our lives! The songs deal with pleasure and pain, disappointment and joy, important people, and the most important of all, God.

THE LORD SPOKE TO HIS PEOPLE THROUGH PROPHETS AT DIFFERENT TIMES IN HISTORY.

JEREMIAH, LAMENTATIONS, HOSEA AND HABAKKUK	Before the nation lost their freedom and before they were taken as slaves into exile, God spoke earnestly with them through the prophets. He urged them to turn their backs on their idols and to faithfully follow Him again. God didn't simply abandon or forget His beloved people. It was their choice to turn away from Him.
DANIEL, HAGGAI AND ZECHARIAH	When the nation was eventually taken into exile, God still didn't forget about His people. He promised that He would return them to their land and return everything they had lost. He promised that His love and care for them would be even deeper than before.
MALACHI	After all this suffering, and God returning them faithfully to their own land, the nation still did not live as God expected of them. Their religious devotion was lacking, and their behavior towards one another left a great deal to be desired.

OBADIAH, JONAH AND NAHUM	There are some books that prophesy about what will happen to the enemies of Israel.

Even though God's own people struggled to remain faithful and obedient to God, that did not give their enemies any reason to rejoice or say bad things about them. They still remained God's beloved people. |
| **ISAIAH, EZEKIEL, JOEL, AMOS, MICAH AND ZEPHANIAH** | The prophetic books don't deal only with the time before and during the exile, some offer hope for a time when the exile would end.

These books contain grave warnings, but also offer great hope for the future. |

IN THE NEW TESTAMENT WE FIND MANY LETTERS THAT WERE WRITTEN BY THE LEADERS OF THE CHURCH TO VARIOUS CONGREGATIONS. THEY TELL US ABOUT WHAT THE CHURCHES WERE EXPECTED TO BELIEVE AS WELL AS HOW THE PEOPLE IN THESE CHURCHES LIVED AND BEHAVED.

ROMANS AND COLOSSIANS	If you've ever wondered what the first leaders of the church, such as Paul, taught, you don't have to wonder any more! He recorded his message, the Good News or gospel, as he liked to call it, in his letters in detail.

GALATIANS, EPHESIANS, PHILEMON, 1, 2 THESSALONIANS

There were also cases where particular churches were struggling with specific issues, such as whether they should still adhere to Jewish rules and customs, or whether Christians had the freedom to behave differently. Could they simply ignore the differences between Jews and non-Jews? How should Christian slaves be treated?

What about Jesus' Second Coming? The leaders of the early church always tried to help by writing their advice and teachings in a letter.

1, 2 CORINTHIANS

New Christians also had a lot of questions about how they should behave. How should they be different when they have become Christians?

1 PETER, PHILIPPIANS AND HEBREWS

Christians didn't always have it easy. Often they experienced hard times and persecution simply because they were Christians. They had to suffer for their faith. Some of the letters that were written by the early church leaders were intended to encourage believers in such circumstances.

Paul drew on a lot of his own life experiences and struggles to show how, with faith in Christ, he was able to persevere through trying times.

2 PETER, JUDE, AND 1-3 JOHN

The early Christians were also not immune to people who wanted to destroy their faith. They often faced confusing and conflicting teachings.

In these situations the church leaders had to step in and set things right by writing a letter to the people.

There are also some wonderful personal letters in which Paul offers advice and encouragement to his younger helpers.

Their lives were certainly not a bed of roses and often Paul had to encourage them and lift them up out of despair.

THE MESSAGE OF

THE BIBLE IN

40 DAYS

BECAUSE GOD IS A GOD OF MERCY, HE ALLOWS THE FALLEN TO RISE AGAIN

Genesis – The Beginning

> "I will establish My covenant as an everlasting covenant between Me and you and your descendants after you for the generations to come, to be your God and the God of your descendants after you. The whole land of Canaan, where you are now an alien, I will give as an everlasting possession to you and your descendants after you; and I will be their God."
>
> GENESIS 17:7-8

The world rolled out of the Creator's hand and it was good (1-2). Unfortunately sin soon hooked its claws into Creation and left indelible marks, especially on the crown of Creation; Adam and Eve.

They became proud and, instead of serving God, they wanted to be God's equals (1-11). Their descendants did not act any differently. They also disobeyed God and hatred and murder soon entered the world. Cain, the first-born son of Adam and Eve, could not contain his jealousy of his brother, Abel, so he killed him (4:1-24).

More and more people turned their backs on God and ended up in the claws of sin. Of course this was very disappointing to God and He sent a huge flood to remind the people of His power. Only Noah and his family survived (6-9).

The merciful God then decided to start all over again – this time with a small group: Abraham and his family (12-25). God made a special agreement (covenant) with Abraham and promised him his own land and a multitude of descendants. Abraham trusted God unconditionally … and he was not disappointed.

God took great care of Abraham and his family. Unfortunately sin was lurking just around the corner. Abraham's grandchild Jacob cheated his brother Esau out of his inheritance. Obviously Esau was furious and Jacob had to flee for his life (26-28). It took many years for God's grace to bring these two brothers together again (29-33).

The twelve sons of Jacob – whose descendants would later become the twelve tribes of Israel – were also not angels (37-50). Typical negative human traits like jealousy, bitterness and deceit were their constant companions. The situation exploded when Jacob singled out his son Joseph as his favorite. His brothers became so jealous that they sold Joseph to the Egyptians as a slave. But the magnitude of God's love and mercy exceeded the hate and sin that became part of human behavior.

Although life in Egypt was difficult for Joseph, he soon discovered that God was with him, even when a woman who had tried to seduce him later falsely accused him of seduction, causing him to land in jail. When one door closes, God opens another. Eventually the "prisoner" Joseph became the governor of Egypt (41:39-46).

During this time Joseph's family was struggling to survive in Israel because of the famine. To survive they had to go begging for food in Egypt. They bowed down low before the governor of Egypt – not realizing that it was their brother whom they had sold as a slave years before. They begged him for help … and suddenly this is no longer the story of Jacob and his sons, but rather a marvelous testimony of God's protection and a way to keep His people together.

The governor, Joseph, embraced his brothers with love. He not only fed them, but also insisted that they all stayed with him.

In this way God's people were reunited, this time in Egypt. God's promises proved to be faithful – He is, and remains, the Lord of history.

A JOURNEY WITH GOD

*Exodus – The Guide that knows
the route and also the future*

> The LORD is my strength and my song; He has become my salvation. He is my God, and I will praise Him, my father's God, and I will exalt Him. The LORD is a warrior; the LORD is His name.
>
> EXODUS 15:2-3

The history, as described in Genesis, ended with the arrival of Joseph's entire family in Egypt. It is here that Exodus, the second book of the Bible, begins.

Joseph's family flourished in Egypt – to such an extent that Pharaoh (the Egyptian king) became concerned about the prosperity of these foreigners in his land. But God was indeed with them.

Pharaoh reacted to their success by treating the Israelites like slaves. Although God remained faithful and was good to the Israelites, Pharaoh made life difficult for them. He gave them virtually impossible building tasks to perform (1-2).

When life became unbearable for them, God appointed Moses as their leader to rescue them from Pharaoh (3-4).

Moses went to Pharaoh with the request to let the people go. Pharaoh refused – who would do all the work? But he did not realize the power of the God of the people whom he was holding captive.

To remind Pharaoh that he was dealing with the living God, God sent plagues to illustrate His power. Only after ten plagues Pharaoh finally gave in and agreed to let the Israelites go.

The Israelites had hardly left when Pharaoh had a sudden change of heart – he wanted them to return! He pursued them with his army and tried to trap them by the Red Sea. Again God came to His people's rescue by safely taking them through the Red Sea. Pharaoh and his men were not so lucky. They all drowned in the sea when they tried to follow the Israelites (5-14).

The Israelites then wandered through the wilderness between Egypt and the land God had promised them for 40 long years. Yet God was with them and provided for them.

When they were thirsty, God gave them water (17) and when they were hungry He provided them with bread (manna) to eat (16). However, the Israelites were often unhappy and dissatisfied, but the grace of God was always sufficient to keep them together.

An important turning point in the history of the Israelites came when they reached Mount Sinai. There God made a special agreement (covenant) with His people (19). He promised them that He would be their God if they would be His people. As His people they should live according to the Ten Commandments (laws) that God had given them (20).

Moses received these Ten Commandments from God on Mount Sinai on behalf of the people. The commandments were written on two stone tablets.

God explained in detail what He expected of His people: they should honor Him, they should observe the Sabbath as a special day of rest, they should treat others with integrity; they were even told how to bring an offering and what the priests were supposed to wear (21-40).

A "Tent of Meeting" (tabernacle) with an altar was built so that they could meet with God in a special way (40). The most significant aspect of being God's people was that God was always with them.

However, this wonderful event also had a darker side. Moses went up Mount Sinai to receive the Ten Commandments. When he did not return immediately, the Israelites jumped to all sorts of conclusions. They thought Moses and his God had disappeared and they felt abandoned. So they made a gold calf to worship and to be their god and leader (32).

Understandably, this faithless act grieved God, but He forgave them because He was committed to His people. God's grace is abundant. This would be proven again and again on their journey, not only through the wilderness, but also in the Promised Land.

Time for team talk

Leviticus and Deuteronomy – The rules of the winning team are discussed

Hear, O Israel: The Lord our God, the Lord is one. Love the Lord your God with all your heart and with all your soul and with all your strength. These commandments that I give you today are to be upon your hearts.

Deuteronomy 6:4-6

God is the God of Israel and they are His people. The agreement (covenant) made at Mount Sinai confirmed this in the book of Exodus. To be God's people of course meant to live and behave like God's people.

God promised to be their God, but they had to be His people in word and in deed. Leviticus and Deuteronomy served as the manual, or blueprint, for their agreement with God. This manual indicated what God expected of them, but it also indicated what they could expect of God.

Leviticus contains regulations dealing with every aspect of the everyday lives of the Israelites. Especially important were the right relations between people and the right relationship with their Lord and God. Their service to God was well regulated: they knew exactly what to offer, and how to make such offerings (1-7).

The priests were responsible for making sure that things went smoothly at the tabernacle (where their meetings with God took place) (8-10). There were also other regulations to keep them pure before God in every aspect of their lives (11-16).

But God was not only interested in their spiritual well-being, He was just as concerned with what happened in their everyday lives. He wanted them to be socially healthy and to reflect His caring nature. He therefore gave them guidelines for behaving properly towards one another.

God told them in detail how husbands and wives should treat one another, how they should dress, how the sick should be treated and gave guidelines for everyday living (17-27). Many of these regulations were even aimed at keeping His people physically healthy: if they ate right and lived right, they would stay healthy.

Deuteronomy does not only contain regulations, it is also an "ancient tape recorder" of some of the speeches Moses delivered to the Israelites. He had to prepare the people properly for the long trip ahead and for their entry into the Promised Land. Deuteronomy also tells about their adventures in the wilderness after they had left Sinai. Deuteronomy's story ends just before the Israelites entered the Promised Land. This was also the time when Moses died (31-34).

Like Leviticus, Deuteronomy focuses on the relationship between God and His people. They can depend on God for everything, because He proved He was a God who keeps His promises. He showed them that He is their Help. He cares for them and protects them. They had to live in obedience and faithfulness to His will (1-30).

God never wanted these regulations to become a burden. He wanted His people to find happiness in living God's way. They should experience joy in doing these things because of their love for their Lord.

These acts of obedience should come naturally since they come from hearts that are filled with love and devotion for their loving God.

God's journal of the journey with His people

Numbers – The story of revolt, love, rebellion and grace

"I am the LORD your God, who brought you out of Egypt to be your God. I am the LORD your God."

NUMBERS 15:41

Egypt, and everything that happened there, was now behind the Israelites. After the events at Mount Sinai, God's people were excited about His promise of entering into the Promised Land. A new future with God lay ahead.

However, between them and the Promised Land, there was still a vast wilderness to cross – and no one really realized how vast it would be ... Nevertheless, they prepared themselves well for their trip, organizing everything thoroughly (1-10, 15, 18, 30).

It was an eventful journey characterized by ups and downs, yet each time they fell, God demonstrated His grace.

The Israelites proved difficult to satisfy,

they were constantly unhappy with the way things were going. They felt that God was not taking proper care of them (11-29) and complained that the food in Egypt had been much better than "God's menu" in the wilderness. When the bread (manna) God provided was not good enough anymore, they insisted on meat. The people kept on grumbling until God sent them quails to eat (11).

But still they were not satisfied. Every now and then they threatened to return to Egypt (to live as slaves again), turning their backs on God and His Promised Land.

It wasn't any easier for the leaders of Israel. God appointed Aaron as priest, but the Israelites thought they knew better and did not spare him their criticism, so much so that God eventually had to intervene. He had to silence the critical tongues by proving that Aaron was the one whom He had chosen.

All those who aspired to priesthood, or thought that they would be better priests than Aaron, had to bring a wooden stick to the tabernacle. Amazingly, the next morning only one of the sticks had budded, blossomed and produced almonds – it was Aaron's stick. Nobody could argue with such conclusive proof of God's approval. It was only then that the Israelites accepted Aaron as their God-appointed priest (16-17).

They tested the patience and grace of God. We read that the situation became so bad that

God contemplated leaving the Israelites in the wilderness. It was up to Moses to salvage the situation so that they could continue (13-14). Yet God is a God of love, patience and grace, and this journey confirmed this even more strongly.

These adventurous times in the wilderness lasted for forty long years. It was a time of learning and formation for God's people. The older generation, who were half-hearted and still idealized Egypt, died in the wilderness (21-25). They never reached the Promised Land.

The younger generation saw things differently. The ghosts of Egypt did not haunt them. Rather, they were driven by dreams of their own land. With their new dynamic leader, Joshua, they eagerly anticipated the challenges and adventures awaiting them in the Promised Land. They knew that with the help of God they would conquer their enemies and the Promised Land would be theirs – and so it was (26-36).

After their long trip through the wilderness they eventually reached the border of the land that God had promised them. There they realized once again that their God is a living God. He is also a trustworthy God who keeps His promises.

A LAND FOR GOD'S PEOPLE

Joshua – God keeps His promises

> It was the LORD our God Himself who brought us and our fathers up out of Egypt, from that land of slavery, and performed those great signs before our eyes. He protected us on our entire journey and among all the nations through which we traveled. And the LORD drove out before us all the nations, including the Amorites, who lived in the land. We too will serve the LORD, because He is our God.
>
> JOSHUA 24:17-18

The Israelites were now ready to cross the Jordan River into the land God had promised them. But it was not simply a matter of moving in and unpacking; it proved to be a considerable challenge. Their road into the Promised Land was paved with conflict and war. The people who already lived in the area definitely did not welcome them with open arms.

We read all about these challenges in the book of Joshua. The first part of the book (1-12) tells of the struggle of the Israelites as they tried to conquer the Promised Land. The second part ends in a climax, telling how each of the twelve tribes of Israel received their own piece of land (13-24).

When setting foot in the Promised Land the Israelites encountered their first obstacle: the fortified city of Jericho. Looking at the strong wall protecting the city they wondered how a group of nomads would be able to scale such a high wall with only a sword and spear? However, in the shadow of that high wall they learned their first important lesson – nothing is impossible for God!

God's people followed His plan and did not attack the city immediately. Instead, God instructed them to circle the city once daily for six days, nothing more. On the seventh day they were to circle the city seven times – and then it happened: the walls of the city crumbled … and it was ready for the people of God to take! (3-6).

This dramatic event shocked the entire area. From then on the other inhabitants of the region were much more cautious of Joshua, his people, and especially of their God.

They entered the Promised Land in triumphant victory (9-12), but not without some adversity, for which they only had themselves to blame.

Every now and then they were so blinded by their success that they thought they had achieved this miracle without God. This proved to be disastrous, as the Israelites discovered when they tried to conquer the city of Ai. Ai wasn't even a strong city. An Israelite by the name of Achan, however, upset the Lord with his disobedience and refused to repent. It was only after the Israelites realized they needed God and repented of their sin and pride, that they triumphed (7-8).

They reached their goal when they conquered the whole land. They divided it among the twelve tribes of Israel. Every tribe (according to the sons of the old patriarch Jacob) was given its own piece of land.

It was a long and eventful road from Egypt to the Promised Land. Therefore the book ends appropriately with Joshua's last words to the Israelites: It is God who made everything possible. Without Him they are nothing and they should remember that.

They should stay close to Him, do His will and serve Him. They should never forget the lessons learned during the journey from Egypt to the Promised Land (23-24). Their lives and their future lay in God's hand.

Human sin and the grace of God

Judges – God's mercy is enough

> Hear this, you kings! Listen, you rulers! I will sing to the LORD, I will sing; I will make music to the LORD, the God of Israel. So may all your enemies perish, O LORD! But may they who love You be like the sun when it rises in its strength.
>
> JUDGES 5:3, 31

God's people settled in Palestine, each tribe on its own piece of land. But their own land did not bring them the blissful future they imagined. The people could not get away from their unfaithfulness, disobedience and sinful nature. What was the problem?

When the Israelites settled in the Promised Land they conquered the land, but did not drive out all the people that were not Jews. They allowed non-Israelites to stay among them in those areas. But these people were not worshipers of the living God of Israel.

They remained loyal to their idols, and again the Israelites fell into the trap of believing that the grass was greener on the other side. The Israelites became infatuated with these foreign idols; they became so tempting to them that God had to warn His people against them many times (1-2).

God did not give up on His people. Instead He made a plan. In times of serious crises, God appointed leaders, or judges, to lead His people out of trouble. These judges repeatedly had to save God's people from the claws of sin and foreign idols.

History repeated itself in a vicious circle. The disobedient Israelites kept on disappointing God. God responded by helping them on the right path, often through punishment and allowing their enemies to conquer them.

A feeling of hopelessness without God would then overpower His people, and they would run back to Him in repentance. Through His grace God inspired judges to lead His people out of their troubles.

This happened time and again. Every time things would improve, but only for a while, until a new wave of disobedience followed and a new judge had to salvage the situation (2-16).

The stories of the various judges differ considerably. They do not have much in common except that their different stories illustrate how God had to save His people repeatedly from the whirlpool of disobedience and trouble. The judges were indeed a diverse group of people, but God used each one in a very special way.

One of the more well-known examples was the fearful judge named Gideon (6-8). God had chosen him to lead the Israelites in their quest against the powerful Midianites. Gideon did not want to know anything about this. In his eyes a war against this powerful enemy was suicide. God had to win Gideon's trust by giving him several special signs to convince him to do his task. In the end, with just a handful of committed men, and with God's help, Gideon came out victorious.

Then there was the strong Samson who had a weakness for women. His life was tainted with disobedience, sin and signs of weakness, but nevertheless God made him a hero of Israel by using him to save His people – despite his weaknesses.

Would this become the pattern for the future of Israel? Was the history of Israel doomed to the vicious cycle of falling and struggling to get up again?

Something drastic had to happen. In the future of God's people there had to be a strong king dominating the heathen nations with their false idols. A beautiful capital city and a temple for the living God were shining on the horizon (17-21).

THE KING WITH

FEET OF CLAY

*1 Samuel – God often
surprises us with His choices*

Those who oppose the LORD will be shattered.
He will thunder against them from heaven; the
LORD will judge the ends of the earth. He will
give strength to His king and exalt the horn of
His anointed.

1 SAMUEL 2:10

Things were not going as smoothly with
the Israelites in the Promised Land as
one would expect. Just as the special leaders
that God appointed to help His people out of
their troubles (the judges) had finished their
work, the Israelites were up to their old tricks
again, doing whatever they wanted.

This, of course was the ideal recipe for sin
and disaster. It was clear that things could not
continue like this. Something had to be done.

God's plan started in 1 Samuel ... with God
helping a childless woman to bear a son. His
name was Samuel and he was a very special

boy. He grew up to become a famous priest and prophet who led God's people through difficult times (1-7). God Himself guided His people by using this special prophet. However, even this did not satisfy the Israelites. They wanted a king on a throne like other nations – one whom they could see and talk to and rally behind when enemies tried to attack them (8).

The people continued whining for a king … and eventually God ordered Samuel to appoint such a king for Israel (9-11). At last Israel had their first king. His name was Saul. Of course, new brooms sweep clean and Saul was no exception.

Initially everything went smoothly. Saul proved to be a good king and an even better soldier. Things were going well, but not for long. Saul started to show weaknesses – he had problems obeying the Lord. Power corrupts and this proved to be true in Saul's case. In his eyes, God gradually became smaller while "Saul, the king" became bigger.

And the bigger Saul became, the less space was left for God. God tried to warn Saul, but without much success. The consequences of this were very serious. Eventually God was forced to do exactly what Saul had done to Him – God turned His back on Saul (12-15).

Again God's prophet Samuel had a message for Saul – this time it was not that he will be king, but that his time as king had run out.

Somebody else would soon sit on the throne. The choice had already been made. The new king would be David, the youngest son of Jesse (16).

David did not immediately take Saul's place. However, things were developing. David started to work at the court as a player of the lyre (a type of harp). His task was to calm the depressed and over-stressed King Saul with the soothing sounds of his music (16:14-23). His talents, leadership, and courage soon gained him great fame among the people.

The whole of Israel cheered him when he fearlessly struck down the giant Philistine warrior, Goliath, with a single stone from a slingshot (17). The people loved David, not only for his courage and bravery, but also for his charming sincerity (18-19, 29-30). So God slowly prepared him to be king and ruler over the people.

Everybody was greatly impressed by David, except King Saul. He started to feel threatened and not without reason. He wanted to get rid of this new shining star. Suddenly David was not welcome at the court any more. He had to flee for his life because Saul wanted him dead.

But David was not like Saul. Saul was full of hate and bitterness, whilst David was not. David actually saved Saul's life several times, demonstrating the integrity of his character (23-26).

This only made Saul even more desperate, to such an extent that he finally turned his back on God for good and consulted a medium. A medium and not God, became his refuge (28). From then on things just got worse.

Saul died shortly afterwards in a battle against the Philistines. His army was overpowered and at the sight of his soldiers running for their lives, he took his own life (31).

This is how the story of the first king of Israel came to an end – it is the story of a king with feet of clay.

A GOOD BEGINNING DOES NOT ALWAYS GUARANTEE A GOOD ENDING

2 Samuel – The beloved king misbehaves

> Is not my house right with God? Has He not made with me an everlasting covenant, arranged and secured in every part? Will He not bring to fruition my salvation and grant me my every desire?
>
> 2 SAMUEL 23:5

The king (Saul) is dead … long live the king! But which king? This was the question on everybody's lips. Although God had already chosen David, the opportunists and opposing factions among the Israelites were far from convinced.

The throne was empty – and more than one person wanted to be the next king. In spite of all their efforts, however, David became king, as God had decided. It did not just happen, it took time, and there were many struggles and bloodshed before he took the throne (1-4).

David was a good king, and this was apparent from the very beginning. His major task was to bring, and keep, the different tribes of Israel together. This was not an easy task, but it had to be done – without unity there was no power.

To accomplish this he took several measures: he made Jerusalem the capital of the kingdom and ensured that the most important religious artifact of the Jews; a large box named the ark of the covenant (the sign of God's nearness); was placed in the city.

On a military level he defeated the Philistines, the arch-enemies of Israel, and established Israel as the major power in that region. His kingdom became stronger and stronger. The Israelites were indeed proud of their new king and he treated them justly (5-10).

The beloved king of Israel also had his moments of weakness, which had a profound impact on his reign. One day, while David was relaxing on the palace roof, he saw a woman bathing and her beauty immediately overwhelmed him. Her name was Bathsheba. But there was one problem: she was already married.

Despite knowing this, David made love to her and she became pregnant. The grip of sin was now closing tighter and tighter around David. He wanted Bathsheba for himself, but he first had to get rid of her husband, Uriah.

That was not too difficult. David simply sent him to the frontline of the war where he was killed instantly. Sin usually multiplies … first there was unfaithfulness, then deceit, and eventually murder. Obviously God was very disappointed and the strong relationship between God and David began to weaken.

Although David confessed his sins and God forgave him, the consequences were severe. Things went wrong where it hurt the most – his family. Bathsheba lost her first baby. Tamar, David's daughter, was raped and humiliated by her half-brother Amnon. Tamar's brother Absalom then took revenge on Amnon by killing him and then had to flee for his life too.

But that was not the end of it. In exile he plotted to take over the throne of his father, David, but Absalom's rebellion failed. For his disrespect David's soldiers made him pay with his life. So we can say that sin has its price.

David spent his last days as a burdened and unhappy man, but God never abandoned him. "I have sinned greatly in what I have done. Now, O LORD, I beg You, take away the guilt of Your servant" (24:10). On his knees the repentant David learned the breadth and depth of God's love and grace.

David learnt that God's grace and love is too great to fathom. He even wrote a song: "The LORD is my rock, my fortress and my deliverer ... my stronghold, my refuge and my Savior" (22:2-3).

God is less concerned about perfection, and more concerned about sincerity. God wants people who stay close to Him in devotion and obedience.

AN EARTHLY
HOME FOR A
HEAVENLY KING

*1 Kings and 1 Chronicles – There
is no other God like our Lord*

Observe what the LORD your God requires: Walk
in His ways, and keep His decrees and commands, His laws and requirements, as written
in the Law of Moses, so that you may prosper
in all you do and wherever you go, and that the
LORD may keep His promise to me.

1 KINGS 2:3-4

After the death of the beloved King David,
God provided a successor to the throne.
His name was Solomon, David's son (1 Kings
1-2). Solomon's reign started out well, he was
sincere and had only the best intentions for
the Lord and His people.

He even fulfilled the dream of his father;
to build a beautiful temple for the Lord in
Jerusalem (5-8). Solomon brought the ark (the
box of the covenant) to the temple. Now the

Israelites could devoutly worship their heavenly King without hindrance.

Solomon became known for his exceptional wisdom (3-4) – it brought him fame far beyond the borders of Israel. Princes and paupers from far and wide, even the queen of Sheba, came to seek his advice and to learn from him. Wisdom such as this could not be found anywhere else in the East or Egypt. His rule was indeed prosperous and blessed.

Unfortunately, there was also a downside to Solomon's rule that ultimately blemished his record. Solomon was known for his many wives (11). They were not the problem, but their beliefs were. These wives came from various regions and countries and brought their idols with them to the palace in Jerusalem.

Solomon knew about these sinful practices yet he allowed them to take place, even in the shadow of the temple of the living God. Sometimes he even joined his foreign wives in offerings to their idols.

This is where things started to go wrong. If the king can do it, everybody can do it! The Israelites started to see these idols through different eyes – they started to look inviting and charming. God was not satisfied with these developments. He sent His prophets to warn His people, but with their eyes on the idols, their ears seemed to be deaf (3-11). Then Solomon died.

After Solomon's death, things started to fall

apart in Israel. Rehoboam, who succeeded Solomon as king, was nothing like Solomon. He was stubborn and did things that were extremely unwise. He autocratically forced his ideas on the Israelites with dire consequences.

The ten tribes of Israel living north of Jerusalem rebelled against this treatment and they declared themselves independent from the administration and rule of Jerusalem. They appointed their own king, Jeroboam, and continued as a separate country.

They were not interested in the temple in Jerusalem and made sacrifices to idols in Bethel and Dan. They had to pay for these sins. Their wicked ways eventually led to disaster (12-16).

The once powerful kingdom of David was now divided into a southern kingdom (Judah and Benjamin) and a northern kingdom (the other ten tribes). In spite of this, God did not forsake them. His prophet, Elijah, was still there, although at times he felt as if he was the only true worshiper left (17-21).

Elijah fearlessly served the Lord in many ways. However, he would be remembered most for his showdown with the prophets of Baal at Mount Carmel (18).

The issue at stake was: who is the real God? Baal or the God of Elijah and Israel? Elijah faced 450 prophets of Baal at Mount Carmel. God humiliated the prophets of Baal and their idol that day. There could now be no doubt who the only true God was.

In spite of this resounding victory Elijah had to flee for his life. Jezebel, King Ahab's wife, was furious and wanted to kill him. Some people never learn. In the end she was the one who was killed. The people of God survived in spite of the odds against them. With God on your side you cannot lose.

This was what the once glorious kingdom of David came to. Fortunately we can learn from their mistakes: If you play with fire, you will burn your fingers. On the other hand, if you stay true to God, you will be victorious.

(1 Chronicles relates the same history, but from a slightly different point of view. The emphasis is on Jewish culture, identity, and especially on the role of the temple.)

IF YOU MAKE GOD'S GRACE CHEAP, YOU WILL PAY AN EXPENSIVE PRICE

2 Kings and 2 Chronicles –
Wrong choices can be fatal

> O LORD, God of Israel, enthroned between the cherubim, You alone are God over all the kingdoms of the earth. You have made heaven and earth. Give ear, O LORD, and hear; open Your eyes, O LORD, and see; listen to the words Sennacherib has sent to insult the living God.
>
> 2 KINGS 19:15-16

Just before his death Elijah appointed Elisha as his successor. Elisha was now God's special prophet among His people (1-2). He was truly a "people's prophet".

He gave new meaning to the expression that God is there for everybody. Whether it was a poor man who had lost a borrowed axehead (6), or the people of a town who needed fresh water, he was always willing to help. He even cured the pagan general, Naaman, who came to seek help from the God of Israel (5). Wherever God needed him, Elisha was a willing servant. His life was a testimony to the fact that God was still working among His people, whether they were rich or poor, young or old, kings or servants.

From a political point of view we see a different, very gloomy story; a story of crises, deceit and disobedience. We read about the different kings (8-17) who reigned over the two kingdoms (the northern kingdom and the southern kingdom).

These kings failed to realize that real fame and success were not counted in the number of battles won or meetings held, but in loyalty to God. They all seemed to fail this test. Because of this, God allowed the powerful Assyrians to take the people of the northern kingdom into exile as slaves.

It is worth mentioning that there were also kings like Hezekiah and Josiah who were quite different (18-25). Hezekiah did his best to do away with pagan worship. He wanted the people of Judah to be loyal to God alone. For a while his efforts were rewarded. However, he also yielded to the temptation of political success, instead of trusting God.

Like Hezekiah, King Josiah tried to bring the disobedient people of God to their senses. He demolished the places of pagan worship and restored the temple of the Lord. He also spared no effort in making sure that his people were living according to God's Law.

However, their efforts were not enough. Although kings like Hezekiah and Josiah tried their best, the Israelites would simply not listen. A few years later, during the reign of King Zedekiah, the Babylonian army attacked Jerusalem and destroyed the temple (25).

Nebuchadnezzar, king of Babylon, led the descendants of King David away into exile. Little was left of the once powerful people of Israel, they were slaves in a foreign land, wondering if God had forgotten them.

But in time the Israelites' situation improved, because God was still their God. The first rays of hope shone when King Nebuchadnezzar's successor released the Jewish king Jehoiachin, from prison. Hope began to rise up among the Jewish exiles and they were not disappointed.

In 538 BC the Persian king, Cyrus, allowed some of the Jewish exiles to return and rebuild the temple in Jerusalem. God had come to His people's rescue and saved them. A new future awaited them.

(The same history is repeated in 2 Chronicles but the focus is on the Jewish culture, identity and especially on the role of the temple.)

NOTHING IS IMPOSSIBLE FOR GOD

Ezra and Nehemiah – Hope does not disappoint

"O LORD, God of Israel, You are righteous! We are left this day as a remnant. Here we are before You in our guilt, though because of it not one of us can stand in Your presence." While Ezra was praying and confessing, weeping and throwing himself down before the house of God, a large crowd of Israelites – men, women and children – gathered around him. They too wept bitterly.

EZRA 9:15-10:1

The books of Ezra and Nehemiah tell the beginning of a new era for God's exiled people. The very people who took the Israelites into exile in the first place, now ordered the Jews to return to Israel to rebuild their old city, Jerusalem, that had been laid to waste.

Ezra was to rebuild the temple and Nehemiah's job was to rebuild the walls protecting the city. Cyrus, the Persian king, even financed their return. With great excitement Ezra and his people arrived from exile at Mount Zion where the temple stood (1-2).

However, the Persian king did not help them out of the kindness of his heart. He knew that Ezra was in debt to him. The far off borders of his territory would therefore be safe and stable.

Ezra's major task was to rebuild the temple. As soon as they arrived at the temple site they started offering sacrifices to God. God proved His mercy and truthfulness to them yet again and opened the doors to a new future for them.

However, it was not all plain sailing. It wasn't long after their arrival that problems arose. There were Israelites who had been left behind when they were taken into exile in Judah (these were mainly people for whom the Assyrians saw no use).

Naturally these people who were left behind took control of the country when the others left. The Gentiles also capitalized on this opportunity and settled in the empty lands of the exiled Jews. They intermarried and created a new land with new people. This is where the Samaritans came from.

When Ezra and his people returned they thought they would be returning to their own country and thought everything would be the same as before. But this was not the case. They had to deal with the "new inhabitants" of their old country and this often led to considerable trouble.

As a result the process of rebuilding did not go exactly as Ezra had planned. They had to cope with the "other people" who demanded to be part of the rebuilding of the temple.

Ezra was not in favor of that. The people who returned from exile did not really want to mingle with them since they did not regard them as pure Jews anymore. Moreover, Ezra wanted to get rid of all the Gentiles and their interests in the land. This obviously caused considerable tension, but with the help of the king of Persia the temple was rebuilt in 516 BC and it was rededicated during a beautiful Passover ceremony.

Nehemiah followed Ezra to Jerusalem. His aim was to rebuild the wall around the city of Jerusalem to protect the inhabitants. The city had to be restored to its former glory. Like Ezra he also encountered much opposition, (1-3) especially when it came to leadership.

He had his hands full with the people from nearby areas who did everything to boycott the rebuilding of the wall. But, like Ezra, this did not discourage Nehemiah. He successfully finished rebuilding the wall around the city (4-7).

Ezra and Nehemiah did not only rebuild the temple and the city, they also restored the spirits and identity of their people. They consciously aimed at leading the Jews to swear allegiance to God and serve Him as they were supposed to (7-13). The Jews responded by confessing their disobedience and turning back to God. Once again His commandments were in their hearts and on their minds. They regained their self-respect and national identity (8).

The history of Ezra and Nehemiah shows that God never forsakes His people and that nothing is impossible for Him. He is the one who can make dreams come true. And when difficult times come, perseverance will be rewarded. Success will follow for those who put their trust and hope in God.

THE WONDER OF A TRUE WOMAN

Ruth, Esther and Song of Songs

The LORD bless you ... Don't be afraid. I will do for you all you ask. All my fellow townsmen know that you are a woman of noble character.

RUTH 3:10-11

The three books Ruth, Esther and Song of Songs have very little in common – except that all three are about women! These books tell about their bravery and loyalty, their beauty and love.

Ruth tells the story of a woman who understood the meaning of loyalty and devotion. Ruth was a Moabite, who married Naomi's son, a Jew. The death of her husband left her and her mother-in-law desolate and alone in Moab. Naomi decided to leave Moab and returned to her native land, Judah.

Ruth had a choice – to go with her mother-in-law to Judah or to stay in Moab among her own people and start over. Out of loyalty to Naomi she followed her to an uncertain future. Those were difficult times for them. But God was with them. He cared for them in His own way.

One day when Ruth was gathering barley in a field, she stumbled across Boaz, the owner of the field. She could not wait to tell Naomi about it. Naomi realized that Boaz was family and family members were obliged to take care of each other. Naomi encouraged Ruth to go look for Boaz again and ask him for help.

Boaz agreed, but did more than what was asked of him – he married Ruth! Suddenly their whole future changed. Indeed, Ruth's love and loyalty made the seemingly impossible possible. If you look at the genealogy of Jesus, you will find Ruth's name there (Matt. 1:5).

The story of the beautiful Esther is one where bravery, loyalty and devotion triumphed amidst hatred, dishonesty and murder. Haman, the chief administrator to the Persian king, devised a treacherous plan to have all the Jews in the area killed on a specific day.

Esther, also a Jew, heard of this plan. Something had to be done! She risked her life by approaching the king of Persia without permission or an official audience and told him about Haman's plan. The king listened patiently to Esther who succeeded in convincing him to help the Jews.

Haman's plan failed and he was put to death because of it. God used the bravery and wisdom of a beautiful woman to save His people. To this day devout Jews still celebrate the bravery of Esther during the Festival of Purim.

Then there is the Song of Songs. It is a collection of songs about the beauty of true love between a woman and her lover. This is a story about the emotions of love that touch us all so deeply.

Two lovers are bubbling with the emotions, excitement and feelings that only true love can bring. They can't stop talking about it and they can't get enough of it either. In the most beautiful images taken from nature they declare their everlasting love for one another.

They cannot endure being separated (3-5). Their intricate and sensitive game of love sometimes drives them apart, only to drive them back even deeper into one another's arms.

Love, devotion, and loyalty make even the smallest and most disregarded people great.

LIFE IS NOT A MATHEMATICAL EQUATION

Job

> "I know that You can do all things; no plan of Yours can be thwarted. You asked, 'Who is this that obscures My counsel without knowledge?' Surely I spoke of things I did not understand, things too wonderful for me to know. My ears had heard of You but now my eyes have seen You."
>
> JOB 42:2-3, 5

People were under the impression that life was predictable – like a mathematical equation. It should be easy to work out: for every good deed you do, God will bless you with something good. By the same token, for every bad thing you do, something bad will happen in return. So, if things are going badly you'd better step up on doing good deeds.

But life is not as simple as that. We learn this in the book of Job. Life is incredibly complicated. In particular, life is not always fair or clearly understandable. Things go wrong; whether you are doing good or bad things; whether you plan thoroughly or not. You cannot manipulate life … this is what the book of Job teaches us.

The story of Job begins in heaven where the Devil said to God that he suspected Job was only serving the Lord to get good things from Him. In fact, the Devil said that Job was not really devoted to God, but rather manipulating the situation to his own benefit. Knowing the real Job, the Lord allowed the Devil to test Job, just to prove how wrong he was.

The Devil was allowed to take every good thing away from Job – except his life. If Job worked on the basis of calculation – good for good; bad for bad – he would lose faith in himself and in God since his manipulative game of calculations will fail (1-2).

So the test began. Job indeed lost everything. While he was sitting on the ash heap, three of his friends came to see him to find out what happened. Job was convinced that he had done nothing wrong, yet things were going very wrong! Their game of "calculating" their good deeds did not seem to be working – how could "good" be answered with so much "bad"?

One after the other, his friends, Eliphaz, Bildad and Zophar, gave him advice. It was clear that they were not convinced by Job's proclamations of innocence – you cannot simply dismiss the calculation game, they thought. Nevertheless, they tried to comfort Job. Eliphaz tried to encourage him not to give up hope and become bitter.

Bildad was convinced that the Lord would not allow those things to have happened to Job if he had not done something wrong – Job just had to confess his sins and his situation would most certainly improve (3-11).

But Job maintained his innocence. Something else had to be wrong and he was determined to find out what. He wanted God to explain why this had happened. His friends were concerned that Job might be too arrogant before God. Elihu actually warned Job not to challenge God, because God is almighty and all-powerful (12-37). Nevertheless Job demanded an answer from God. So, by grace, God granted Job his wish to meet with Him (38-42).

Interestingly enough God does not provide quick answers to Job's questions – He does something completely different. He decides to show Job who He really is. He shows Job His Creation, the sea and mountains, the animals in all their variety. This was a strange way to answer Job's question about why things went so wrong. But gradually Job started to understand how great God is.

God is not simply another person, He is unlike any other. He does not think like us, neither does He act like we do. He is far greater than any person and could therefore not be degraded to a mathematical equation. His actions cannot be calculated and neither can He.

Instead of trying to manipulate, calculate or explain God, we should rather sit in humility before Him – faithful and trusting; not rebellious or manipulative. Neither God nor life can be explained or mathematically calculated. In truth the only way to live a life of abundance is in complete dependence on the God of life.

Job had to learn that life was not a mathematical equation; neither is God. Life may go wrong for even the most faithful child of God, since life is unpredictable and uncertain. But that does not leave believers defenseless. Because God's love, grace and unequaled power never change!

SONGS FROM GOD'S SONGBOOK

Psalms – Prayers from the heart

The LORD is my shepherd, I shall not be in want. He makes me lie down in green pastures, He leads me beside quiet waters, He restores my soul. He guides me in paths of righteousness for His name's sake. Even though I walk through the valley of the shadow of death, I will fear no evil, for You are with me; Your rod and Your staff, they comfort me.

PSALM 23:1-4

Living our lives in the presence of the Lord touches our deepest emotions because it touches our very existence. And what better way to express our emotions than through song and prayer, whether we are happy or sad, whether we are praising or grieving?

This is what the Psalms are all about: singing, praying and rejoicing in the Lord. There are 150 psalms that take us on a journey through all the different emotions and prayers that grew out of believers' hearts years ago.

In Psalm 1 we are introduced to the three main characters of Psalms: God, the people who serve God, and those who don't serve Him. Good people do not stand in the circle of sinners, but journey through life with God and consequently they prosper.

On the other hand godless people waste their lives on their way to total destruction. Like chaff in the wind they are blown away. The choice presented in Psalms is quite simple – which group do you belong to on your journey through life?

On a long trip any traveler needs a map. Without it he or she is lost. The same is true of the journey of life. Without God's Word; the light for one's feet and the map for one's journey, life becomes uncertain and without purpose. It is therefore appropriate that many psalms sing praises about the wonder of God's Word and the joy that it brings: "This has been my practice: I obey Your precepts" (119:56).

If you follow God's Map on your journey, He promises to travel with you. God is your travel companion. This is a good reason to rejoice: "Praise the LORD. Praise the name of the LORD; praise Him, you servants of the LORD" (135:1). His kindness and love are celebrated in song over and over again: "Give thanks to the LORD, for He is good. His love endures forever" (136:1).

In Psalms we can see that it is pure joy to go on such a journey with God. Just to know that you are cradled in His hand and that He will take care of you is enough to help you face any challenges that life might throw at you: "You have assigned me my portion and my cup; You have made my lot secure" (16:5).

You can be assured that you are never alone, because God is with you and He listens to you: "When I called, You answered me; You made me bold and stouthearted" (138:3). Even when you make mistakes, the Lord does not abandon you. His grace, love and forgiveness are overwhelming: "For You have delivered me from death and my feet from stumbling, that I may walk before God in the light of life" (56:13).

There are even psalms that wonder about God, and allow you to complain when things are not going well: "Why, O LORD, do You stand far off? Why do You hide Yourself in times of trouble?" (10:1). But one should never fall into the trap of doubting the Lord.

God will help you; He will change your woeful complaint into a song of praise: "I will be glad and rejoice in You; I will sing praise to Your name, O Most High. My enemies turn back; they stumble and perish before You" (9:2-3). Yes, "In God, whose word I praise, in God I trust; I will not be afraid. What can mortal man do to me?" (56:4).

These are but a few of the festive colors of

the rainbow of song and praise found in the Psalms. There are also songs about the temple and the king, about searching for wisdom, and about God's judgment and omnipotence.

Yes, in the Psalms we discover a gold mine of praise, emotions, hope and gratitude. These treasures are available to every person wanting to explore the Psalms.

A WORTHY LIFE HAS
STYLE – GOD'S STYLE

The wisdom of Proverbs

He whose walk is upright fears the LORD, but he
whose ways are devious despises Him.

PROVERBS 14:2

L ife is a game, a serious game. Like any
other game it has rules. The question is:
How do you play the game of life? Which
rules should you follow to make a success?
Well, God gave us a Manual, and one thing is
certain, if you want to know how something
works, consult the Manual.

Proverbs is filled with daily wisdom that
will enhance your life with color and excitement, purpose and pleasure. It contains real
secrets for a good life. There are longer poems
(1-9) as well as shorter expressions (10-29).

Proverbs is not about ivory tower wisdom,
it offers advice on the hustle and bustle of
everyday life. It talks about family relationships, sex, your responsibility towards others
and their responsibility towards you. Even is-

sues like laziness and dishonesty do not escape the magnifying glass of Proverbs. Children are encouraged to obey their parents and young people are warned against the snares of immorality. Proverbs also does not hold back any praises when it comes to the ideal woman (31). Just about every topic is addressed.

The golden thread that runs through Proverbs is this: Everything in life begins and ends with God. God created everything and by watching the wonder of Creation we learn so much about Him.

Creation mirrors God as orderly and great, as a lover of harmony and peace, as a sustainer of life, hating everything that destroys or hinders life. To a certain extent Creation reveals much of God's Manual for a purposeful life. Watching ants can be a good lesson for lazy people, while eating too much honey might just cure the greedy.

Hence, if you want to play the game of life wisely, you have to play it according to God's rules; the rules that are found in His Manual. His rules should become your guidelines. That is also why Proverbs draws such a sharp distinction between wise and foolish people.

Good people are those who live according to God's will, do their duty and search for harmony and peace. Foolish or evil people are those who ignore God's rules. They are lazy and do not respect others; they lie, cheat, envy others and are unfaithful in times of trouble.

Living with them is like crossing a river on a greased pole – you never know where your next step will take you. This is not what God wants for us.

Although Proverbs warns against the dangers in life, it is not negative towards life. You should not be like a scared hare, running away from everything out of fear of doing something wrong.

No, life should be lived to the full. If you can do a good deed, do not wait. Just do it! If you can bring joy and pleasure to somebody, you should do it. Nothing will be achieved through laziness or bad habits. Rather pick a piece of dry bread with a clear conscience than a house stacked with delicious food wrapped in constant fighting (17:1). A happy heart, joy and cheerfulness make life worthwhile.

Proverbs is clear about the way that we should play the game of life: put God and your relationship with Him above all else. Follow His Manual and do what He asks of you. If you do that, you will walk the path of wisdom.

LIFE IS FOR
LIVING ... ENJOY IT!

Listen to the wisdom of Ecclesiastes

When I applied my mind to know wisdom and
to observe man's labor on earth – his eyes not
seeing sleep day or night – then I saw all that
God has done. No one can comprehend what
goes on under the sun. Despite all his efforts to
search it out, man cannot discover its meaning.
Even if a wise man claims he knows, he cannot
really comprehend it.

ECCLESIASTES 8:16-17

Ecclesiastes is a book that contemplates
the true meaning of life. When can one
honestly say that life is worth living? The
king of Israel – as the author introduces himself (1:12) – was a seeker, setting out to find
answers to what the purpose of life was.

Perhaps success in life was the ultimate
answer? Well, our author passionately started
out pursuing success, and he achieved great
success! He looked back on the majestic build-
ings of Jerusalem, plantations and fruit trees,

large herds of animals, a vault full of treasures and servants ready to obey his every order. He achieved more than any ruler before him.

But when he looked around him at all his achievements, he could only say, "Yet when I surveyed all that my hands had done and what I had toiled to achieve, everything was meaningless, a chasing after the wind; nothing was gained under the sun" (2:11). There was no permanency, no lasting satisfaction in his achievements – it was like chasing after the wind and ending up with nothing.

What about money or wealth? Surely there must be satisfaction in these? The author soon learned that money is a ruthless master. The more you have, the more you want – you just can't get enough. And the "friends" your money brings you, care more about your money than they care about you.

The moment your money disappears, those friends also disappear. Again the author's conclusion was: "As a man comes, so he departs, and what does he gain, since he toils for the wind?" (5:16).

Our author continued his search without finding a satisfying answer. He tried many other things, like pleasure (2:1-3) and fame (4:13-16), but each time the meaninglessness of what he had sought after brought him to the conclusion that it is nothing more than a chasing after the wind.

What exactly is "life"? Watching the best-prepared athlete or the strongest army lose against all odds brought our author to the conclusion that life is not fair, nor does it owe us anything. There is a time for everything no matter who you are; a time to laugh and to cry; a time to be happy and to be sad; a time to be born and to die. Yes, death awaits us all. It doesn't matter who you are, life sweeps you along in the stream of good and evil.

Even if life is sometimes unpredictable or unfair, never stop living. You should not waste a single moment of your life! You should live life to its fullest, come what may. Whatever hand life deals you, you should play it enthusiastically.

If life deals you a bad hand, make the best of it. And if life deals you a good hand, play just as passionately. But most importantly, says the author of Ecclesiastes, use every opportunity God gives you to live fully. Do not let life pass you by. If you have pretty clothes, wear them, if not, wear what you have; and if you only have a dry piece of bread, enjoy it as if it is a plate filled with gourmet food.

While you are young, enjoy your youth before old age comes. Yes, enjoy life with those whom you love, before it is too late. Accept everything with gratitude from God.

Asking too many questions about life will just frustrate you. And you'll soon discover that there are more questions than answers. Accept the mysteries and puzzles of life, because more often than not your attempts at trying to unravel the mysteries will lead you on a never-ending journey.

There are many things that you will just never know, and you should accept that. One thing you do know is: You can trust God, because He knows everything. And He knows best.

With God on your
side life will never
be a dead-end street

Isaiah

A voice of one calling: "In the desert prepare the way for the LORD; make straight in the wilderness a highway for our God. Every valley shall be raised up, every mountain and hill made low; the rough ground shall become level, the rugged places a plain. And the glory of the LORD will be revealed, and all mankind together will see it. For the mouth of the LORD has spoken."

ISAIAH 40:3-5

The prophet Isaiah was one of God's greatest messengers in history. If we could ask him what the essence of his message to God's people was, what would he say? He would say that his message is to encourage us to focus our attention on the only true and living God. A God who never lets His people down – no matter how difficult times might be. He is a God of life and new beginnings. Even if sin seemingly maneuvered His people into a dead-end street, it was this graceful God who offered His people a way out, towards a new future.

The prophecies in this book cover three important periods in the lives of God's people: before, during and after exile. Each of these times in Israel's history represented a unique situation that had to be addressed through the words of the prophet.

Before the exile, the people of God became arrogant and felt that they didn't need God (1-39). This was a major mistake, as they soon discovered. You cannot play games with the Author of life, the one who is all powerful. God had a covenant with His people that obliged them to serve Him, or else they would be punished. God could not simply overlook their blatant disobedience.

God mobilized the big world powers in Isaiah's day, the Assyrians and the Babylonians, against Judah. Their presence cast an ominous cloud over Judah that burst into a devastating storm. However, these world powers could not mobilize themselves as they were only instruments in God's hands. And so God used these world powers to punish Judah for their unwillingness to serve Him.

Hence God's people ended up in exile. During exile the people realized that their living God did not reject or forget them. His presence gave them hope (40-55). It would not be long before God would lead them home again. He used the seemingly powerful Persian king, Cyrus, to facilitate the return of His people out of exile, and back to Jerusalem.

These powerful acts of the Creator God stood in sharp contrast to the idols of the Babylonians who were feeble and powerless. How can one even think of comparing idols cut out of wood to the powerful, living God who holds history in His hands?

Back in their ancestral homeland, after their exile, the people of God had a future again. Out of the ashes of the old city of Jerusalem, a new temple and city would arise. In this temple they would serve God while God Himself would sustain and protect them.

The light of hope was shining brightly for them, the future was inviting, and life was calling out to them. Yes, God's people were back in Judah (56-66). Unfortunately there was the constant danger that the people of God would start wandering off to idols again. This was something they could not afford to do, so Isaiah encouraged them to keep trusting in God.

On the road to exile and back, one thing stood out clearly: God is a God of life and hope. He is indeed the only true God. His salvation is not only for a special few, but for everyone. In God they should put their hope and build their future.

With God there is
hope, even in
hopeless situations

*Jeremiah and Lamentations –
Never forget to take God seriously*

"This is the covenant I will make with the house of Israel," declares the LORD. "I will put My law in their minds and write it on their hearts. I will be their God, and they will be My people. No longer will a man teach his neighbor, or a man his brother, saying, 'Know the LORD,' because they will all know Me, from the least of them to the greatest," declares the LORD.

JEREMIAH 31:33-34

The prophet Jeremiah ministered before and just after the fall of Jerusalem (626-586 BC). These were troubling times in Jerusalem that caused the message of Jeremiah to be an emotive mixture of warning, condemnation, and hope.

Jeremiah pleaded with the people to turn back to God, otherwise God would punish them. After all, they had made a covenant with God and it was their responsibility to keep that covenant, otherwise they were in danger of losing the temple and their territory would be destroyed.

The people did not believe Jeremiah because they thought that God would not allow this to happen. After all, He was seen as the Protector of Jerusalem and the temple was His! He would never abandon His temple.

They argued that losing His temple would be a sign of weakness, and not a sign of God's punishment. It would suggest that heathen idols were stronger than the God of Jerusalem. Surely God would never allow that! So they regarded the prophecies of Jeremiah as empty.

This way of thinking gave Judah a false sense of security. They simply continued in their old ways, doing whatever they wanted; they were masters in playing the "religious game". They regularly visited the temple on the Sabbath and offered sacrifices according to the "rule book", but that was the extent of their devotion to God.

In their day-to-day life, there was no place for God. They deceived each other, exploited the poor, robbed and murdered. During the week they even visited the altars of heathen idols, where all kinds of immoral acts were on their to-do list (1-13). They did not really comprehend that God was not interested in their sacrifices to Him. God was more interested in them as committed and devout people –

in their obedience to God, and their service to Him (7).

After ample warnings God's patience ran out. What Jeremiah prophesied eventually happened. The enemy overwhelmed Jerusalem and broke down the temple. God, the One who controls people and histories, used the king of Babylon as His instrument to punish the Israelites.

Because He is God, He could do this, and in fact, He could do what was right and good to win His people's hearts. He could cause something new to grow out of their punishment, because God's punishment does not equal rejection. It is always a righteous and just expression of His love to cleanse and purify people.

Thus, God wanted to make a fresh start with His people. He would change their attitudes and make it so that His commandments would be imprinted on their minds. He would send His Spirit to lead them in doing His will. Being in exile did not spell the end. In fact, the rays of a new beginning had already begun to shine in the darkest hours of their exile.

Then there is the book Lamentations (by Jeremiah – although it is not clear whether he is the author of this book or not). It is a collection of five songs written after the fall and destruction of Jerusalem. In these songs the raw, undigested grief of Judah is apparent.

Judah felt abandoned and defenseless, like a widow who knows no consolation (1). These five songs contain sad questions about where God might be and why His grace had not been enough to cover the sins of Judah (5). The songs, however, radiate confidence and the certainty that God will raise up those who have fallen (2-3).

Jeremiah and Lamentations serve to remind the faithful to cherish hope, even if the situation looks bleak. Those who have faith, have hope.

WITH GOD PUNISHMENT FOLLOWS SIN, AND GRACE FOLLOWS PUNISHMENT

Ezekiel – with God you can always start over

> "I will give you a new heart and put a new spirit in you; I will remove from you your heart of stone and give you a heart of flesh. And I will put My Spirit in you and move you to follow My decrees and be careful to keep My laws. You will live in the land I gave your forefathers; you will be My people, and I will be your God."
>
> EZEKIEL 36:26-28

The Lord appointed Ezekiel around 593 BC as a prophet to call His disobedient and idol-worshiping people to repentance (1-3).

Ezekiel had a vision in which he saw the Israelites in Jerusalem serving idols in the temple. Right at the very entrance of the temple an image of a Babylonian idol, the size of a man, confronted the worshipers. Apart from that there were twenty-five men in the temple worshiping the sun with their backs turned to God.

This was how far His people had fallen. These false worshipers also showed their fallen state with regard to their behavior and treatment of one another. People were lying to, and deceiving one another; they were loveless, fighting over everything. You could not tell that they were God's chosen people.

Ezekiel had no other message for them other than to repent. Otherwise God would take Jerusalem and the temple away from them (6-7). Despite all Ezekiel's efforts and warnings, the people of Judah ignored him and continued in their old ways.

Eventually God made a decision that had dire consequences for the people of Judah. God decided to leave His temple, His city and His people. These disobedient people were on their own, God was no longer there to protect them. This meant the end of the city, because without God's help Judah could not take on their mighty enemy, Babylon (8-11).

Jerusalem and the temple were soon conquered and destroyed, not because of the strength of the Babylonians, or their wooden idols, but because it was the punishment from God for their disobedience (11-24).

As exiles in Babylon the Israelites learned an important lesson. They realized that their God is not one of many gods. He is the only true and living God. His power does not only extend over Israel, He commands all the powers and kingdoms of the earth.

If He needs to use the Babylonians to enact His will, He will do so. And when the Babylonians became too arrogant, He punished them too. No, the God of Israel is no ordinary god. He is the all-powerful God who holds everything in His hands.

But punishment and rejection are not the same thing. The Lord never rejects His people completely. He is the Lord of life, hope and new beginnings (33-48). He does not like to punish His people, and if He does punish them, it is to open their eyes to the destruction caused by their own disobedience and thus to draw them closer to Him. He wants them to live.

That means living according to the will of the Giver of all life. This is the only way that they can share a new future – a new beginning, with God on their side (36-37).

Indeed, God promised a new future to His people. He would lead them back from exile to their beloved country where they would rebuild Jerusalem and the temple. But this time it would be more glorious and beautiful than before. It would be a New Jerusalem, God's Jerusalem, from which life would flow, reviving the whole world. All the people and kings of the earth will gather and bow down before the God of Israel.

Yes, God will be among His people and they will be His people by serving and obeying Him. He will be their God and they will be His people.

What lions understand but humans do not – God is king!

Daniel – The writing is on the wall

> Praise be to the name of God for ever and ever, wisdom and power are His. He changes times and seasons; He sets up kings and deposes them. He gives wisdom to the wise and knowledge to the discerning. He reveals deep and hidden things; He knows what lies in darkness and light dwells with Him.
>
> Daniel 2:20-22

The book of Daniel tells about great heroes of the faith. Apart from some prophecies in the latter part of the book, Daniel tells of a few Jewish exiles who stood up for their faith in God against the earthly superpower of their time; the Babylonian empire.

From a human point of view their situation looked bleak, but these heroes were never disheartened, because they knew they were not alone – God was with them.

In Him they trusted. And if you are in God's hands, you are in safe hands, even if the storms of despair rage against you.

The story of our heroes (1-6) begins in the palace of the Babylonian king where Daniel and his friends were working. The king chose the cream of the young men of the land. Physically, they had to look great. So the king let them eat royal food from his kitchen. In spite of the temptations, Daniel and his friends remained faithful to the Jewish food laws that God had given them.

It became obvious after a while that Daniel and his friends were healthier and intellectually sharper than the others because they followed "God's diet". To choose God's way is always the right choice.

Then Daniel got his big break! King Nebu-chadnezzar had a dream about a giant statue that was shattered and he wondered what this dream meant. All his wise men tried to explain it, but no one could clarify the meaning of this strange dream ... except of course Daniel who interpreted the dream with the help of God. The king was impressed.

Just as things were improving for Daniel and his friends, the king built a huge golden statue and ordered everybody to worship it. Daniel's friends, who were there too, refused. They only worshiped one God and He was the Lord their God. Such behavior could not be tolerated by the king and he threw Daniel's three friends into a blazing furnace. Then something amazing happened: They were not burned to ashes. They did not even have a burn mark on them. Even in the flames of a blazing fire God protected them (3).

After King Nebuchadnezzar's death, Belshazzar became king of Babylon (5). One night in a drunken rage he tried to degrade and dishonor the living God. He proposed a toast to the idols, using the cups and bowls that they brought from the temple in Jerusalem.

While they were drinking, a human hand suddenly appeared and began writing a message on the wall. No one could understand the message. It was certainly not a favorable message to the king: God decided not only that his time, but also the time of his kingdom was up.

During the reign of the next king, Darius, Daniel's biggest test lay ahead. The king decreed that only he should be worshiped. Daniel disobeyed him fearlessly. In spite of the king's orders, he continued praying regularly to the living God.

As punishment for his disobedience to the king (and obedience to God) Daniel was thrown into a pit of hungry lions. Then another amazing thing happened: The lions did not attack Daniel or tear him apart. They lay peacefully at his feet. What a miracle! After that no one could possibly doubt that Daniel's God was the only true God (6).

God never lets down those who serve and obey Him. The message of Daniel can be summed up as follows: God's children do not escape the furnaces and the lions' den, but when they do have to enter them, they're never alone. God is with them!

WHERE IS GOD?
GOD IS HERE!
WHERE ARE YOU?

Hosea, Amos, Habakkuk and others –
The prophets before the exile

> Though the fig tree does not bud and there are
> no grapes on the vines, though the olive crop
> fails and the fields produce no food, though
> there are no sheep in the pen and no cattle in
> the stalls, yet I will rejoice in the LORD, I will be
> joyful in God my Savior.
>
> HABAKKUK 3:17-18

God's people never have to wonder where He is – He is always with them. Even if they lose sight of Him, He never lets them out of His sight. And He does not want them to be in the dark about what He wants. He even sent two prophets (Isaiah and Micah) to His people simultaneously to reassure them of His presence and love.

Sadly, not even this helped. God's people seemed to be deaf and blind to His ways and were unwilling to listen to Him. Too often they looked away from God with their eyes sparkling for the idols of their time.

This idolatry saddened the Lord. His people did not want to listen to the warnings given by His prophets. Hosea preached in a different way – not only with words, but also through bold actions. God wanted to illustrate to His people what they were doing wrong, and show the pain and suffering it was causing, so He asked Hosea to marry a prostitute. She was never faithful to him and constantly left him for other lovers.

This was exactly what Israel did. They were always flirting with idols while they actually belonged to God. Hosea warned the people in word and deed – they were going to lose everything. To lose God is to lose all.

However, there was still hope. Although Israel was unfaithful and deserved nothing but death, God remained faithful. Because God was there, a spark of love, grace and hope remained. Much like Hosea's unfaithful wife who eventually returned to him, Israel would eventually return to their Lord. Rays of hope also shone through the messages of other prophets like Micah and Zephaniah.

Even though they warned the people of God's impending judgment upon them for their disloyalty, this judgment would not mean the end for them. Rather, it was part of God's plan for a new beginning for them.

Amos had a difficult task. He had to convince the people that they faced serious problems while they thought everything was fine. They had a stable government, they were economically successful, and it even seemed to go well with the "church". But this was only on the surface. God's eyes saw everything.

The people were mistreating and exploiting one another. Flashy clothes were more important to them than the person who wore those clothes. They could not be bothered about anyone else but themselves. The only things that mattered were their own wealth and status. It was Amos's task to warn them that this was not the way God wanted His people to live.

Then there were prophets who were searchers in difficult times because they did not have all the answers; they were searching for God. Habakkuk, for instance, wrestled with the question, "Where is God?" It seemed to him that God's people were getting worse by the day. Why does God allow this? Through intense struggles Habakkuk eventually found an answer. Situations may be unfair and uncertain, but God is never unfair.

You can trust God in any situation, come what may. Even if the fig trees do not bud and the animals die in their stalls, you can still rely on God.

God is, and will always be a God of love and grace, whatever the situation may be.

GOD IS NOT SATISFIED
WITH HALF-HEARTED LOVE

Joel, Zechariah, Haggai, Malachi

"They will be Mine," says the LORD Almighty, "in the day when I make up My treasured possession. I will spare them, just as in compassion a man spares his son who serves him. And you will again see the distinction between the righteous and the wicked, between those who serve God and those who do not. Surely the day is coming; it will burn like a furnace. All the arrogant and every evildoer will be stubble, and that day that is coming will set them on fire," says the LORD Almighty.

MALACHI 3:17-4:1

The exiled Jews knew what it was like to lose everything: their territory, their temple, their freedom. As exiles in far away Babylon they yearned for their land at the foothills of their beloved city, Jerusalem.

God made this dream come true for them. They were allowed to return from exile to Israel to rebuild their temple in Jerusalem. They returned with great excitement and expectations, but their enthusiasm did not last long. The reality they had imagined was very different to the reality they encountered.

In fact, at times things went so wrong that while they were rebuilding the temple they had to work with a shovel in one hand, and a sword in the other! Through these circumstances the prophets Zechariah and Haggai tried to encourage and motivate the people not to lose faith, but to stay focused. They had to continue worshiping God, and God alone.

Wasn't it true that God had promised that He would be with them in Jerusalem? This gave them every reason in the world to rejoice and be happy. Eventually everybody, including all the other nations, will join in worshiping their Lord in Jerusalem.

The prophet Joel also tells much about the day when Jesus will come to live among His people. Everyone, young and old, will be filled to overflowing with His presence and power, especially when His Spirit comes upon them.

Then they would be truly free and their hearts would overflow with joy and happiness. In the meantime, the Israelites just had to stay true to the Lord and worship Him alone, because He is God Almighty who is and will always be in control of everything.

When Malachi began his ministry, the Jews had finished rebuilding the temple (516 BC). You would have thought that they would be content and happy, but that was not the case. They thought that everything would go their way, especially since they rebuilt the temple to worship God. Nevertheless they were constantly hit by droughts and other adversities. This confused them to the point where they wondered where God was.

Malachi gave them a "God's eye view" of what was really happening. It was not God who had changed or refused to keep His promises. It was the people who had forgotten their agreement with God. They were not keeping their end of the bargain.

In fact, they were not even doing the basic things to keep God happy; like giving Him what was rightly due to Him. Instead of giving their best to Him, they were doing their best to give as little as possible. Obviously God was not satisfied with this half-hearted love.

So, it was not God who had turned His back on them; they had turned their backs on God. If they were only willing to turn back to God they would be able to see and experience His love. They would see Him waiting with outstretched arms, eagerly anticipating their return.

You can't lock God up in temples, or hide from Him

Obadiah, Nahum and Jonah – God is not only interested in His own people

He prayed to the LORD " ... I knew that You are a gracious and compassionate God, slow to anger and abounding in love, a God who relents from sending calamity."

JONAH 4:2

God controls history. Not only the history of His own people, but also the history of the whole world. As we've already seen, even the superpowers of the world were only instruments in God's mighty hand.

God could close His hand at any time and everything would be over. God's love and grace are therefore also meant for these superpowers. But if they challenge God, they will experience His wrath.

The book of Jonah illustrates this point very clearly. God commissioned Jonah to warn the Persians in Nineveh of God's impending judgment. To bring such a message of doom to the capital city of your enemy was a bit scary, to say the least! As a result Jonah tried to run away from God, but without success (1).

He had to learn the hard way. After a close call in a shipwreck, Jonah landed in the belly of a fish. There, in the depths of the ocean, he experienced what it felt like to be far away from God. Jonah soon realized that life without God is empty (2). He did not try to run away again.

He obeyed God's wish and went to Nineveh with the message that God intended to punish their godlessness. The message spread through the city like a wildfire and the people recognized their sinful ways. Even the king repented of his sins before God (3).

God saw their remorse and decided not to punish the city. Jonah's ego was bruised by this – it made him look like a false prophet. What he had said did not happen. But in a gentle way God explained to him that the people of Nineveh were just as much a part of His Creation and perfect plan as the people of Israel. God has enough grace for everybody.

The prophet Nahum's (625-612 BC) message is clear: If a nation becomes too arrogant and starts playing god, they will quickly realize who the true, living God is. They will learn the hard way that God is stronger and more powerful than they thought. They will discover that it is God, and not humans, who controls the kings and their kingdoms. All power belongs to God. This is the lesson that Nineveh, the capital city of the mightiest power of ancient times, had to learn.

They thought they were invincible and could do whatever they wanted. But they quickly realized just how wrong they were – they could only do what God allowed them to do.

Then we meet Obadiah, the prophet who had to proclaim the end of Edom, Israel's neighbor and archenemy. God's vigilant eye misses nothing in the universe. He immediately spotted the people who had become so haughty that they dared to ridicule God's people. The people of Edom had gone too far and God had to punish them. Edom burnt like dry grass.

Yes, God is a mighty God – His love is endless, His grace is endless, His patience is endless, but you should not think that you are mightier than God! If you do, you will quickly realize your mistake.

ISRAEL IS FREE AGAIN, BUT ONLY FOR A LITTLE WHILE

The period between the Old and New Testaments

The last historical accounts in the Old Testament are the stories of Ezra and Nehemiah who returned from exile to rebuild Jerusalem and the temple. After that a historical silence fell on the biblical narratives lasting approximately 400 years. This silence was broken by the history of a baby born in Bethlehem.

What happened during those 400 silent years to the people of God? Many dramatic things happened and were recorded in 1 and 2 Maccabees, the so-called Old Testament apocryphal or deutero-canonical books. In this way we can know what happened in the 400-year period between Ezra and Jesus' birth.

When Ezra returned to Jerusalem, Persia was still ruling the world, this rule even extended to the Jews who had returned to Israel. Persia's reign was ended by a Greek named Alexander the Great in 333 BC. Alexander conquered the whole of the Persian Empire, which meant that the Jews had to pay their honor and taxes to the new Greek rulers.

The Jews were not happy about serving foreign Greeks in their own country, but there was little they could do about it. One day the Greeks went too far. The successor of Alexander in the Jewish areas, Antiochus Epiphanes IV, targeted their religious activities. He wanted them to worship Greek gods instead of the true God, and consequently ordered unclean animals to be sacrificed on Jewish altars. He even erected a statue of the Greek god Zeus in the temple.

This was too much for the Jews to handle. Under the brave leadership of Judas (with the nickname Maccabeus, which means "the hammerer") and his brothers, God's people started resistance movements against the blasphemous Greeks.

Shoulder to shoulder and with great bravery they defended God's honor. No sacrifice was too much for them. They left their homes, lived in caves in deserted mountains and started a guerrilla war.

Judas was an excellent leader and general for the resistance armies. He led the Jews from one victory to another. In the end the Greeks had enough and turned the territory and the temple over to the Jews. For the first time since their exile, the Jews were free to rule themselves. In 164 BC they could once again worship their God in His temple without hindrance.

This freedom and peace lasted for a hundred years – and then the Jews ruined it for themselves. Two of the leaders were competing against each other. One of them, Hurkanus, thought he was clever and concocted a plan to outwit his opponent, but instead he made a fatal error. He approached the Romans, who were by then in the direct vicinity of Judah, and asked them to help him become the high priest. In exchange for the high priesthood he would allow them free access into Israel.

This is how the Romans entered Jerusalem – without shooting an arrow or casting a spear. They simply took the territory for themselves. In 63 BC the Jews again served foreign masters.

When the biblical (New Testament) history continues, Israel is under Roman rule. But a Kingdom was on its way, it would be ruled by a very different King – Jesus of Nazareth.

THE GOOD NEWS (I):
THE MESSAGE THAT
CHANGED THE WORLD

*The first part of Jesus' story as
told by Matthew, Mark and Luke*

"Do to others what you would have them do
to you, for this sums up the Law and the Prophets."

MATTHEW 7:12

The Good News of God had a humble beginning. An ordinary girl, Mary, became miraculously pregnant through the Holy Spirit,
and Jesus was born (an event we comme-
morate on Christmas Day each year, although
Christmas Day is not His exact date of birth).
Of His childhood we know little, except for
the visits by the wise men and the shepherds
just after His birth (Matt. 1-2; Luke 1-2).

The story starts again thirty years later
when Jesus commenced with His public ministry by preaching and performing miracles.
He was baptized by John the Baptist and He

began to preach and tell the people about God. This was why God had sent Him, and the people hung on to His every word.

The message of Jesus Christ was simple yet powerful: "Repent and turn back to God, since God, the King of the universe, is among you." Years later His disciples would testify that being with Jesus was like seeing, hearing and experiencing the presence of God among them (1 John 1:1-2).

He preached anywhere and everywhere the wonderful Good News of God, whether it was in a house, the temple, next to a lake, on a mountain, under a tree, or on the road. His sermons were revolutionary and powerful.

In His famous Sermon on the Mount (Matt. 5-7) Jesus explained how valuable human beings are. Humans are invaluable to God and so they should treat one another with appreciation and respect. Honesty, forgiveness and servitude were some of the qualities that God wanted to see among His people. These qualities bring about true healing and are life-giving. People are not supposed to hurt one another, either physically or emotionally, even if the other person is considered their enemy.

Destroying someone's reputation, or exploiting his or her heart and mind is just as bad as killing him or her with a knife. The golden rule Jesus gave was simple and straightforward: do to others what you would have them do to you.

Jesus was a master storyteller. With beautiful stories (parables) He graphically explained the gospel (Good News) of God to those who wanted to listen. For example, He tells about a rebellious young man who left his father's home and ignored his responsibilities.

Alone in a far away land, after squandering all his money, he realized his mistake. He returned to his father, willing to serve as a slave, as long as his father was prepared to take him back.

Back home his loving father awaited him with open arms. This parable is actually about our loving God whose arms are wide open for every person, every sinner, who wants to return to Him (Luke 15).

But Jesus did not only preach. He also performed many wonderful miracles. He healed people, drove out demons, and even multiplied food and walked on water. However, He did not go around like a magician arranging shows or playing tricks. No, on the special occasions when He did perform a miracle, it was a "sign" of the power of God working through Him.

It was proof that God was with Him; how else could these wondrous deeds be explained? Showing God's presence through these miracles also underlined the truth of what Jesus was saying. He was sent from the one true God and so His message is also true.

Jesus' message deeply touched the lives of many people. Soon people were following Him in faith. But everybody did not share this excitement. You can read more about this in Day 26.

THE GOOD NEWS (II):
THE FINISHING LINE ...
AND A CROSS

The stories about the crucifixion and resurrection of Jesus as told in the Gospels of Matthew, Mark and Luke

"For even the Son of Man did not come to be served, but to serve, and to give His life as a ransom for many."

MARK 10:45

The first part of the Gospels tells a success story. Large crowds followed Jesus to drink in His every word and to watch Him heal the people. But there was also another side to the coin. Soon it became clear that not everyone was as excited about Jesus. Especially not the religious leaders of the time. He became a real threat to them.

Why would anyone possibly want to turn against Jesus? Well, initially Jesus preached in Galilee that was far north of the religious capital Jerusalem. In Galilee people were eager to listen to His message, even non-Jews. However, as Jesus approached Jerusalem – the seat of Jewish religious power – the opposition against Him grew.

The most important reason for this opposition was Jesus' openness and honesty about the way religion had been distorted in the religious powerhouses of the Jews. What should have been a living and lively relationship between God and His people had been turned into a morally corrupt game of blindly obeying laws.

This became apparent in Matthew 23 where Jesus accused these leaders of being hypocritical. In their religion everything revolved around themselves, their laws, and their power, while God was forgotten.

This criticism did not go down well with the religious leaders and they decided that Jesus had become too big a liability. If He carried on like this their religious system and comfort zone would be destroyed. He had to be eliminated (as their ancestors had done with numerous prophets before Him).

The sparks really began to fly during a Passover feast in Jerusalem. When Jesus entered Jerusalem the ordinary folks greeted Him like a king, singing in celebration.

The next day Jesus went to the temple and drove the businessmen with their goods, intended for offerings, out of the temple area. They were not interested in God, but only in the profits they could make. They had turned the temple into a common market place.

Naturally the message of Jesus appealed to the ordinary folks who realized what was going on. The religious leaders in Jerusalem felt that Jesus was gaining too much popularity and was also interfering in their religious lives.

They could see only one solution – to get rid of Jesus. Behind these efforts to eliminate Him and silence His message were the powers of evil. It was not only a local conflict in Jerusalem, but a conflict of cosmic proportions.

Jesus was captured with the help of one of His own followers, the disciple Judas, who betrayed Him. On that same night, Jesus was brought to trial before the Jewish council (Sanhedrin). Early the next morning they sent Him to the political leader of that area, Pontius Pilate, with a request that He should be put to death.

Pilate listened patiently but could find no evidence of Jesus' guilt. He conveyed this to the Jews who refused to take no for an answer. They insisted that Jesus had to be killed. Eventually Pilate yielded to the pressure. Jesus was crucified on Golgotha on that same day, and later that afternoon He was buried in a nearby grave.

The leaders in Jerusalem thought that this would be the end of the "Jesus story". What they did not realize was that this was only the beginning of God's new plan with mankind! The death of this one special Man brought life to the whole world. Jesus died on the cross for the sins of all mankind. "My God, My God, why have You forsaken Me?" (Mark 15:34) He cried out before He died for our sins. Three days later, His tomb was empty. He had risen from the grave!

Everybody could clearly see that this was the work of the God of life. How else could a person rise from the grave? This message of resurrection and new life would become the heart of the faith and the confession of believers throughout the centuries.

God had resurrected Jesus from the dead and in the same way, everybody who believes in Him will be resurrected from death to eternal life.

THE GOOD NEWS (III):
A LOVE STORY WITH NO BOUNDARIES

The story of Jesus according to John

> "For God so loved the world that He gave His one and only Son, that whoever believes in Him shall not perish but have eternal life."
>
> JOHN 3:16

The Gospels tell the story of the Good News of Jesus. As early as the second century, people tried to summarize the four Gospels in one. But the Christians wouldn't fall for it. Who Jesus is can't even be described properly in four Gospels, let alone one.

Like a diamond glittering in the sun, the diversity of Jesus' person and message glitters uniquely in each of the different Gospels, each one adds richness to His message by describing Him from a unique perspective.

In the gospel of John it is the divine side of Jesus as the Son of God that glitters most brightly. This Jesus has been with His Father since before Creation. Their relationship is so close and special that John described them as being one (10:30).

Yes, Jesus is not only with God, He *is* God (1:1, 18). Of course this means that by looking at Jesus we can learn who God is and what He plans for us. No wonder this Gospel started by calling Jesus "the Word" – which is God's way of talking to, and communicating with us (1:1).

God sent Jesus, His Son, into the world to live among ordinary people (1:14; 3:16). The gospel of John is about a family feast – about the lost children who can be reunited with their Father and be with Him in His house forever (14:1-2).

This evangelical message is divided into three sections. The first message tells of Jesus' great love for all the people in the world (1-12). In the second section we learn about Jesus' relationship with His disciples, (13-17) and the final section focuses on the importance of the Cross (18-21).

The message of Jesus to this world is a divine message overflowing with love. God loves this world and wants everyone to become His child (3:16).

This was radically different from what the religious leaders of that time preached – for them, only "good people" who obeyed their rules were religious. Jesus preached a different message: God loves everybody, whether an important Jewish leader (3) or the least important person imaginable (4). For God there was no distinction. Membership to God's family was open to all.

The Jewish leaders became jealous of Jesus because the ordinary people eagerly embraced this message of love. As a result they decided to get rid of Him.

Realizing this, Jesus gathered His loyal followers at a special meal to encourage them for the times that lay ahead (13-17). He encouraged them by telling them that when He returned to His Father they would not be left as orphans. The Holy Spirit would be with them as their special Helper. He would comfort and help them.

They would live as God's family in this world, witnessing the power of Jesus and His message of love. This witnessing was not only to be a testimony of words, but the people were to show love and compassion to one another so that other people would be able to see Jesus' love shining through them into the world. Yes, whoever believes in Jesus will receive eternal life.

But there was another side to the message of Jesus – whoever does not believe will experience the wrath of God (3:36). The love of God comes with one loving condition – it must be accepted as it is offered in the person of Jesus.

John's story about Jesus is a story of love;

a love that draws people closer to God; a love that overpowers darkness and sin; a love that binds God's children together and overflows into this world.

It is a love that is there for anyone to accept. It is a love that can make you a child of God.

THE WORLD BECOMES GOD'S PULPIT

Acts – The church expands

> "You will receive power when the Holy Spirit comes on you; and you will be My witnesses in Jerusalem, and in all Judea and Samaria, and to the ends of the earth."
>
> ACTS 1:8

The message of Jesus rapidly became world news. It all began in Jerusalem, after Jesus' ascension. He was glorified and taken up into heaven.

Shortly afterwards, on the day of Pentecost, God's power was spectacularly illustrated when His Holy Spirit came to fill the hearts of every believer. And what a show of godly power that was! The lives of the believers were dramatically changed!

Filled with the power of God they were no longer afraid to witness about what Christ had done for them. Death could not even scare them from proclaiming the Good News of the resurrected Jesus. Yes, the floodgates of the power of the Holy Spirit had been opened.

Through the power of the Holy Spirit believers became truly effective instruments in the hands of God. Just look at Peter. He must have been astonished at the success of his first sermon; after he had preached literally thousands of people became followers of the risen Christ.

This was the same Peter who had denied Christ just a short while earlier, but now he was truly revived through the presence of God's Spirit in him (2-3).

The church grew rapidly in Jerusalem and this bothered the religious leaders as they thought they had put an end to the "Jesus story" by nailing Him to the cross. The people were flocking after the risen Jesus and as a result they went back to their old tactics: get rid of the "threat" by silencing the Spirit-filled witnesses.

The religious leaders became so violent that they stoned Stephen to death because he was a Christian (7). Christians had to flee for their lives to escape the same outcome.

But what seemed like a misfortune for the Christians was actually a blessing in disguise. The Christians who fled in different directions took the gospel with them. The Good News was not only heard in the streets of Jerusalem, but from the mountains of Samaria, the plains of Asia Minor and the marketplaces of the capitals in the ancient world. The world was on fire with the Good News of Christ.

Much of the contents of Acts is about the life of the apostle Paul. God appointed him as messenger of the gospel to the non-Jews in Asia Minor (Modern Turkey), Greece and even Rome. He went on three major journeys (known as his three missionary journeys) from city to city, fearlessly preaching God's Good News.

His message was clear and simple: the living God of the Old Testament raised Jesus, the Messiah, from the dead, to show that God's new future had dawned. This gives hope of new life to every person who believes in Him.

As was the case with Jesus, some people opposed the truth of this message and they mocked Paul, beat him and threw stones at him. Yet all these hardships could not prevent Paul from fearlessly spreading the message of hope.

Towards the end of his last great journey, Paul visited Jerusalem. There he was thrown into jail by a group of hostile Jews. Paul ended up in Rome, the capital city of the known world and it is here where Acts ends.

What we do know is that Paul's arrival in Rome emphasized the fact that the rapid spreading of the gospel could not be stopped. Even in the streets of the capital city of the ancient world, the Good News of God echoed.

The world is God's pulpit and the sermon about His Good News is inspired by the Holy Spirit Himself.

NOTHING CAN SEPARATE YOU FROM GOD'S LOVE

Romans – Paul's "Testament"

> I am convinced that neither death nor life, neither angels nor demons, neither the present nor the future, nor any powers, neither height nor depth, nor anything else in all creation, will be able to separate us from the love of God that is in Christ Jesus our Lord.
>
> ROMANS 8:38-39

Romans is one of Paul's last letters. One may even call it Paul's "testament". In other words, it is a summary of the Good News he so desperately wanted everybody to hear. He wanted people to realize that they are in dire need of God, that God can change their lives and can give them a new life, a new future and a great hope.

The letter starts with a basic problem that is common to all people: reluctance, and even refusal, to listen to God and obey His will. Some people are so full of themselves that there is no place left for God. Thus, they deprive themselves of His presence. They gather all that they can to try and get along without God. But the more they try to live their own lives without God, the deeper they sink into sin and alienation from God (1-3).

Is there a solution? Yes, turn back to God. The only catch is that once you've appointed yourself as the ruler of your life, it is difficult to give that prime position back to God again. Indeed, if you allow sin to get a hold of you, the grip is firm (3).

Fortunately no grip is too firm for God to break. Jesus is a specialist in breaking the power of sin. Jesus restores, He revives, and He even has the power to give hope in a hopeless situation.

Through His death and resurrection He not only broke the grip of sin, but also did everything necessary to restore every person's relationship with God if he or she is willing to bow at His feet.

Paul explained this wonderful plan of restoration and atonement in terms of a court case. Sinners cannot enter into the presence of the heavenly Judge as if nothing has happened. With all the sins we commit every day the Judge need not even think twice before finding us guilty!

But the heavenly Advocate, Jesus, steps in and manages to overturn this verdict for everyone who believes in Him. How does He do this? He intercedes on our behalf. Because of what Jesus did, we are acquitted in court (8:33-34). Yes, through Jesus a person can change from a guilty sinner to a free child of God. We can all be assured that nothing can separate us from the love of Jesus, because, if God is for you, who can possibly be against you? (8:31-36).

Becoming a child of God changes your status in the eyes of God forever. The verdict is clear: you are no longer a sinner, but God's own child. What an incredible gift that is!

God's children are clothed with all the beautiful gifts that God gives and can experience grace, joy, peace, hope, the glory of God and most importantly, love (5).

They soon realize that being God's child is never a singles game – you and the Holy Spirit are playing the game of life together. Playing this game in close union with Him has huge advantages – He guides you through the highs and lows of life, protects you when you are weak and speaks to God on your behalf when your words seem to dry up. It is not only a matter of getting a new life, but getting a powerful and joyous life.

With a "match partner" who gives you so much grace and love, you simply cannot play the game of life as if you are the center of everything. You must put your life in God's hands if you join in this adventurous match with the Spirit (12:1-2).

He will focus your attention on the others

around you (12-15). His love for you must become your love for others. Through His grace you must become gracious towards others. When others need you, you must be available; whenever love is lacking you have to supply that love.

Whether you live or die, you belong to God. He will give you all the grace that you need – more than enough to share with others. This is how a believer should live – today and every day.

GOD'S GIFTS MAKE
YOU RICH – BUT ONLY
IF YOU SHARE THEM

Paul's first letter to the Corinthians

Now these three remain: faith, hope and love.
But the greatest of these is love.

1 CORINTHIANS 13:13

Paul's message to the people in Corinth was simple: Jesus was crucified, but He has risen from the grave (1-2, 15). They received the Spirit of God who came to live within them. As spiritual people (*Gr = pneumatikoi*) they were inspired by the Spirit, sensitive to His spiritual wisdom and guidance (2).

But now what? What must a person do when he or she becomes a Christian? At least they knew that they had to practice what they preached. Since they now preached about Christ, it meant that they should practice His presence in, and through, their daily living. But what does that mean for their everyday lives?

In his letter Paul addressed practical issues that they were struggling with.

Firstly he gives guidance to the congregation on how to work together. They spent far too much energy fighting and arguing about things that didn't really matter (1-4). They should forget about their own interests and rather focus on God and on seeking His will for their lives.

It is like working in a garden – the one plants and the other waters, but in the end it is only God who can make the plants grow. One person can't say that his contribution is more important than the other's. Without God whatever they did would not mean a thing.

To know one's unique place in a congregation was so important to Paul that he repeated the importance of co-operation by comparing the congregation to a body and its different parts. Members of a congregation each have their own place and task. Only if they all work together and each one does his little bit, will the body be healthy and strong. Even though the eye and foot differ, they still need each other (12). The one cannot claim greater importance than the other.

God does not think one child is more important than another. Thus, spiritual pride has no place in the Christian's vocabulary. Christians have no choice but to help and support one another. They should be loyal to one another; patient and kind, full of forgiveness, without envy or boasting. They should not bear grudges or keep records of wrong things done against them simply so that they can retaliate. This is what love boils down to – it always protects, perseveres, and hopes (13).

Corinth was an immoral place. Some people just did what they wanted to. Paul reminded the congregation of the special care God took of His flock through His Holy Spirit.

The Spirit is the constant companion of the congregation, inspiring, guiding, and helping them. One way of doing this was by giving them spiritual gifts. These gifts were intended to strengthen and empower the congregation.

He compared it with giving a child medicine and good food in order to keep the child (congregation) healthy and strong. In the "medicine box" were spiritual gifts like spiritual wisdom, sound spiritual judgment, an attitude of servanthood, healing, and even doing miraculous things. The Spirit was there to give the congregation what they needed when they needed it (12-14).

Paul concludes his letter with a message of hope for the future (15). Jesus was raised from the dead, showing that there is life after death, and that God has the power to overcome death. This gives believers hope for the future: they know that God will raise them from death to live with Him forever. What a wonderful future to look forward to!

DO NOT STAND IN THE WAY OF GOD'S POWER

Paul's second letter to the church in Corinth

"My grace is sufficient for you, for My power is made perfect in weakness." Therefore I will boast all the more gladly about my weaknesses, so that Christ's power may rest on me. That is why, for Christ's sake, I delight in weaknesses, in insults, in hardships, in persecutions, in difficulties. For when I am weak, then I am strong.

2 CORINTHIANS 12:9-10

The people of Corinth were quarrelsome at times. The moment Paul turned his back, the members of the church began to slander him. He wrote this emotional letter to his fellow believers in Corinth (55-56 AD).

He was extremely upset about it as these were the very people he shared the Good News with. Paul's friends Timothy and Titus resolved the problem and things went back to normal. In the letter he addressed a number of issues.

Children of God could easily argue that nothing should go wrong with them, since their heavenly Father should take care of them. Yet, after his experience with the people of Corinth, Paul was acutely aware that being a Christian was not all moonshine and roses. On the contrary, things go wrong and life can be hostile and difficult at times, even for a faithful believer.

Paul does not deny, or try to reason away the problems that Christians encounter, but he emphasizes the fact that believers can always count on the power and presence of God.

He uses a lovely image to explain this marvelous truth: The earthly life is like a cheap jar of clay that can easily break. Yet, there is a valuable treasure inside the jar – and that treasure is the power and glory of God.

The believer should not have his view obstructed by the jar of clay, but should rather enjoy the wonder of the eternal treasure it contains. It is the faithful presence of God, and not our earthly struggles, that makes life worthwhile for all eternity.

Paul also carefully explained how one can become a child of God: "If anyone is in Christ, he is a new creation; the old has gone, the new has come!" (5:17). Jesus is the one who restores, renews and gives life. The sins of humans shatter their perfect relationship with God. However, with Jesus we can make a new beginning. Jesus restores our relationship with God by reconciling us with our heavenly Father (5).

Of course, every relationship requires an effort from both sides. Believers should not receive this wonderful gift of God's grace in vain (4-5). As new creatures they should live new lives. They should care for one another. When the poor Christians in Judah were in need of help, their brothers and sisters in Corinth should have come to their aid.

Paul does not ask for tithes, as was the Jewish custom. No, if you belong to God, more is expected of you. God does not want money from you. He desires the hearts and the love of His children. The currency of love is not expressed in money but in selfless devotion to God and His people.

Sure, this includes money, but it asks for much more. When other believers are in need, you should help them, even if it requires much more than your tithe. Jesus gave everything for those in need, and those who follow Him should do the same (8-9).

In the last chapters of this letter Paul showed what was going on in his heart (10-13). Very often life did not go his way. One could almost wonder if God was on Paul's side if one looks at all the difficulty he had to endure during his life. But Paul knew that God's love and grace would never forsake him. No, God's power works differently. Paul could not achieve anything on his own, but if he allowed

God to work through him, the world would be shaken by God's power. God's power was made perfect in Paul's weakness (12:9). It is not your circumstances that are important, but the way you choose to act within those circumstances that matters.

God's love for you is not measured on the barometer of how good or bad things are going. Rather, it is measured by God's presence in your life and His relationship with you that nobody can take away. Even if things take a bad turn, He is still there for you.

THE SPIRITUAL OXYGEN THAT LETS YOU BREATHE FREELY

On laws and freedom in Galatia

> Know that a man is not justified by observing the law, but by faith in Jesus Christ. So we, too, have put our faith in Christ Jesus that we may be justified by faith in Christ and not by observing the law, because by observing the law no one will be justified.
>
> GALATIANS 2:16

One of the first congregations that Paul established was in the province of Galatia (more or less in the center of modern-day Turkey). Naturally, this was also the congregation to whom Paul addressed one of his first letters.

This became necessary, since they struggled with a particular problem. They had recently become Christians and were not sure what exactly was expected of them. Now that they were Christians, should they still obey the law as they did when they were still Jews? Was this still what was required in order to please God? Should they still obey the Jewish laws, as they did in the Jewish religion?

Paul approached this problem carefully. He knew that it would be his word against the word of others. So he established his authority to speak on this subject by first telling them a bit about himself.

He emphasized that the message that he preached was not of his own making, he had received it directly from Jesus (1-2).

It was Jesus Himself who had called and equipped him for His work. As a result he urged the congregation to trust him and not tolerate false apostles. These false apostles would only mislead them with their false teachings.

The Jews believed that the only true way to God was through meticulously keeping the Jewish law in its smallest detail. However, Paul told them that this was not the road to God, not because there was something wrong with this road, but simply because people were not capable of staying on the road. People were constantly losing their way by breaking the laws and doing wrong things. This would mean that no one would ever find their way to God.

Jesus showed us a different road. The road of faith in Him (5:1), in other words, walking with Him and following closely in His steps.

The law no longer determined your relationship with God. Faith did that.

If one looks at Abraham one can see that he trusted and believed in God, and because he believed, he was called God's friend (3:1-14). He did not need the law for that. Likewise, faith in Jesus makes you a friend of God. This shows the power of true faith. From this power each believer can live.

It means that Christians are free if they believe in Jesus. They no longer have to follow laws slavishly to try to impress God. No, their lives and behavior are now driven by their friendship with, and love for, God. It's not obedience to the laws, but a loving heart that should dominate their thoughts and actions; this would make them truly free.

On this road of freedom the Holy Spirit is their constant companion, guiding them on their journey with God. It is not slavery to the law, but the freedom of the Spirit that is the answer (5).

This freedom does not mean that believers can do whatever they like. No relationship works like that. Being in a relationship with God means honoring the relationship, not because there is a law that requires you to, but because love compels and motivates you.

That is why Christians are under the control and guidance of the Spirit of God. He leads them on the road of service to God (5:13-26). This road passes by the fountains of love, kindness, patience, goodness and peace (5:22). Through the inspiration of the Spirit, believers drink from this fountain and pass it along to others so that they can also have a taste of love and freedom.

A RACE YOU CAN'T AFFORD TO LOSE

Paul's letters to the Philippians and Philemon while in prison

I can do everything through Him who gives me strength.

PHILIPPIANS 4:13

On his first visit to Philippi, Paul was thrown in jail because not everybody liked the gospel he preached. That night the jail doors miraculously swung open – God was at work. Everybody, including the jailer, realized that God was with Paul and was working through him (Acts 16).

Years later, while Paul wrote this letter he was behind bars again. But this time the jail doors did not open. They stayed shut. What happened to Paul's "godly power"? Had God abandoned him?

Paul answers this question with a testimony: "I can do everything through Him who gives me strength" (4:13). It is not a matter of God's power abandoning him, but rather a matter of His power strengthening him to endure whatever hardships came his way. The power was still there, just in a different way.

The power of God works in various ways. When necessary, it can open jail doors. But at other times the doors might stay closed while God's power explodes around them.

Paul explained that he befriended the guards while he was in prison. As other Christians heard of this, they began to grow in confidence preaching the gospel. Suddenly the gospel was spreading fast all over.

The "jail doors" swung open in a different way. The fear that "locked" Christians up, and prevented them from testifying about Jesus was gone. One person was behind bars so that many others could be free to spread the Good News about Jesus (1:12-14). Paul's closed cell doors had nothing to do with the absence of God's power. God just had another way in mind of using His power to work in people's lives.

But what was this special apostle of God's secret? The secret in Paul's life was simply that he knew Jesus Christ as his Lord, and this truth surpassed everything else (3:7-11).

Nothing could be more important than this. Through his faith in Jesus he knew for sure that he would attain righteousness with God, and be raised with Christ to abundant and eternal life.

To explain this he uses the imagery of an

athlete. He runs with determination like an athlete, not looking back, so that he can run into the arms of God (3:12-4:1). There he feels safe, since that is where his future lies. His power and determination come from the presence and promises of God.

Therefore, neither a dark jail cell nor the slander of others could discourage him. He knew that he was running through the power of God and that God was on his side.

In another of Paul's letters he addressed Philemon, who was an important member of the church at Colosse. We again see how God powerfully opened "jail doors" in the lives of people.

Philemon's slave Onesimus had run away, a deed that was punishable by death at that time. Through circumstances Onesimus landed in jail with Paul, and Paul helped him to run into the arms of Jesus. This is where Onesimus discovered freedom and a new life. He was indeed set free from his jail of sin.

This was not the end of the story. Onesimus was a Christian now and had to do the right thing. He had to return to his earthly employer, Philemon – even if the cost was death.

But Philemon received him back in love and not with a whip. After all, the behavior of freed people should mirror what Jesus taught them – to be loving and forgiving people.

CHRISTIANS PLAY THE GAME
OF LIFE WITH NEW RULES

*Paul's letter to Colosse
and the people in Ephesus*

Whatever you do, whether in word or deed,
do it all in the name of the Lord Jesus, giving
thanks to God the Father through Him.

COLOSSIANS 3:17

Colosse was a religious city, perhaps a bit
too religious. They were always accepting
new religious ideas, mixing them with their
own and ending up with "religious stew".
What boiled up from this religious stew was
the conviction that every person was responsible for his or her own salvation. If you wanted
to get to heaven, you would have to do it yourself.

But it was not that easy – between a person
and heaven were many spiritual powers and
agents who blocked the way to God. However, one could manipulate them in different
ways, allowing one to get closer and closer
to God. It was like climbing a ladder: Each

spiritual power or agent you succeeded in manipulating meant another step closer to heaven. (Read Col. 2:8, 16-23 to see how they were to climb these steps).

Then these people heard the message about Jesus and they put Him into the "religious stew" too! According to them He was just one more step on the ladder to heaven, yes, one more spiritual power to manipulate. The Christians were not sure what to do with this way of reasoning from their fellow citizens in Colosse, so Paul came to their rescue.

They first had to understand who Jesus is. He is definitely not another step on the ladder to God. He is much more than that. He is the Creator who created all these powers and what's more, He created the whole world. He is not just one of them. He is the one closest to God, Jesus is God's beloved Son, to whom God has given the fullness of His glory.

To reach God you do not need to climb spiritual ladders, or manipulate spiritual powers. With Jesus, the pathway to God is simple. You must believe in Him, because if you are with Him, you are also with God.

Even if sin has damaged your relationship with God, Jesus can fix it (1:13-23). How He does that is carefully described in Colossians 2:6-19. Jesus gives the fullness of God that is in Him to every believer. It simply means that the believer becomes what God wants him to be because Jesus changes him accordingly.

Since He is the Creator, He can also recreate sinners into new people. He cleanses them from sin and destroys the power of evil that threatens them. They no longer carry the status of sinners in the eyes of God, but rather the status of victors who partake in His triumphal procession through this world.

If Jesus has made you a child of God, you dare not keep on playing the game of life according to the Devil's rules. You cannot ignore who you are – a new creature, clean from all sin, living in the fullness of God.

You must bring who you are in line with what you do. What is important to Him should be important to you. Everything you do or say should be done according to the will of Jesus (2:20-3:4).

The will of Jesus is no secret (3:5-4:6). A believer should get rid of bad things such as lust, evil desires, bad attitudes, anger, malice, quarrelling, lying and deceit.

They should discard these things like dirty clothes. Only then can you put on new, clean clothes of love, peace, kindness, humility, and patience.

Paul's letter to the people in Ephesus is often called an expansion of Colossians, but with one extra emphasis: Paul simply cannot stop talking about the power of the grace of God that breaks down all barriers between people.

God does not only welcome some people;

He welcomes everybody. It does not matter who you are or where you come from, you are welcome.

In God's sight all people are equal. Indeed, in His church there is only one group of people: His people. There you are free to be what you truly are, His beloved child.

BE PREPARED – THE LORD IS COMING

1 and 2 Thessalonians – Paul's first letters

They themselves report what kind of reception you gave us. They tell how you turned to God from idols to serve the living and true God, and to wait for His Son from heaven, whom He raised from the dead – Jesus, who rescues us from the coming wrath.

1 THESSALONIANS 1:9-10

The letters to the congregation in Thessalonica were the first letters that Paul wrote. After establishing the congregation on his second missionary journey, Paul went on to Athens and Corinth. In Corinth he grew worried about the congregation (1 Thess. 2:1-16) and wrote a letter to them to find out how they were doing (1 Thess. 2:17-3:3).

The thing on everybody's lips was when and how Jesus would return (Acts 17:3; 1 Thess. 1:9-10). The Thessalonians were waiting eagerly for this to happen and it seemed to have been a major topic of conversation. The people in Thessalonica wondered about four things in particular:

✝ They wondered what was going to happen to believers who had died before the Second Coming of Christ. Since they were already buried they would not be able to join those who were alive and ready when Jesus came for them.

Paul reassured them that God will not forsake anyone – not those in the grave nor those who are alive. God will first raise the dead who believed in Christ and then all the other believers would meet Jesus to be with Him forever. No one would be left behind (1 Thess. 4:13-18).

✝ They were curious about the exact date of Jesus' return; they wanted to mark the day on the calendar. Paul explained that nobody except God knows the time and day when Jesus will return.

What we do know is that His return will be sudden. Believers should not be caught off guard, but they should be prepared and ready for His return (1 Thess. 5:1-10).

✝ The Christians were the minority in Thessalonica and because they were different, the other inhabitants of the city often made life difficult for them. But they could rest assured, when the Lord returned, things would change.

God would punish those people who rejected the Good News and did not want to bow their knees before Him. Those who did not believe in Jesus would experience God's full wrath when He came to earth again (2 Thess. 1:5-10).

† Some of the believers in Thessalonica were so excited that they were swept away by stories that Jesus had already returned. This left the poor Christians puzzled. Paul came to their rescue, explaining to them that they should be alert: the Devil is constantly trying to mislead God's people.

False stories will do the rounds; and there will be even more false stories in the years to come. The Devil will do everything he possibly can, even spectacular things, to try and convince people that they should not worship Jesus, but rather worship him. Believers should not allow themselves to be deceived by these lies.

When Jesus returns all those attempts and shows of power will be swept aside by a single breath of the Lord (2 Thess. 1-12).

Paul also gave the people a few guidelines for their everyday lives. Of course, they were not always sure how a Christian was supposed to live, since they had only been Christians for a short while.

It is for this reason that Paul explained to them that they should love one another, keep on doing good things (1 Thess. 4:1-12; 5:14-25), respect their leaders (1 Thess. 5:12-13) and gave other practical bits of advice. He assured them that in doing these things they would be ready when Jesus returned.

A LIFE UNDER NEW MANAGEMENT – GOD'S MANAGEMENT

1, 2 Timothy and Titus – Paul the pastor

> You, man of God, flee from all this, and pursue righteousness, godliness, faith, love, endurance and gentleness. Fight the good fight of the faith. Take hold of the eternal life to which you were called when you made your good confession in the presence of many witnesses.
>
> 1 TIMOTHY 6:11-12

Paul's "children in faith", Timothy and Titus, were his closest friends and pillars. They worked as a team spreading the Good News from town to town and country to country. They were also the people whom Paul could rely on to stay behind and help new congregations find their feet, while he continued on his journey preaching the gospel.

Being part of Paul's team was not always easy for these young friends of Paul. People are sometimes jealous and bitter, even though they are Christians. Timothy and Titus learned this the hard way. They were often criticized by the very same members of the congregation they were supposed to serve. They were criticized for being too young, or that their preaching was not sound. Sometimes they just became the target of difficult people who loved to quarrel and fight (1 Tim. 6:3-5).

However, both Timothy and Titus learned that they could count on Paul's loving support. Paul's letter to them addressed the root of the problem – false teachers who were trying to confuse the congregation with lies and false teachings (1 Tim. 6:3-5; 2 Tim. 3:1-9).

Obviously, the Devil's main aim is to prevent God's Good News from spreading throughout the world. As long as the Devil has this plan, Christians will continue to experience opposition and hardship. These hardships will mostly come in the form of people who fight and quarrel about everything. They constantly try to discredit the sound message of Jesus by entangling it in such a web of lies and confusion that people don't know what to believe any more (1 Tim. 6:2-5; Titus 3:8-11).

Therefore, Paul's timely warning: difficult times lie ahead for Christians since God, His message and His people, will become very unpopular in this world (2 Tim. 3:1-9). When that happened, Christians like Timothy and Titus should not lose heart even if their circumstances are not always easy. They should endure everything and stand by the message of faith and hope in Jesus.

In light of these difficulties that await Christians, Paul summarized the following message so that they could know the truth: Jesus came into this world to redeem sinners (1 Tim. 1:15; 2:5-6; 3:16).

Timothy and Titus should not be afraid to proclaim this message, even though they were young. It is not their age, but their message that counts. They should watch their lives and doctrine, fighting the good fight for their faith (1 Tim. 6:11-21; 2 Tim. 2:1-7).

There were not only problems with false teachers. The Christians were also unsure about how to organize themselves as a church, so Paul gave them good advice on how to build up and organize their congregations.

The elders and deacons should be good leaders. In general, the members of the congregation should be consistent in their way of living and should always behave like children of God. There should be no discrepancy between who they are and what they do as children of God (1 Tim. 2:8-3:13; 5:17; Titus 1:6-9; 2:1-15).

On a personal note, Paul reminded his young colleagues of God's grace that is enough for him and would also be enough for them (1 Tim. 1:12-20). They should stay close to God and put their hope in Him (1 Tim. 4:10).

Follow the Map to heaven ... Never become tired

Hebrews tells one how to stay on the winning side

Therefore, since we are surrounded by such a great cloud of witnesses, let us throw off everything that hinders and the sin that so easily entangles, and let us run with perseverance the race marked out for us. Let us fix our eyes on Jesus, the author and perfecter of our faith, who for the joy set before Him endured the cross, scorning its shame, and sat down at the right hand of the throne of God. Consider Him who endured such opposition from sinful men, so that you will not grow weary and lose heart.

Hebrews 12:1-3

With so many different religions around, it is little wonder that people get confused. How can one be sure one's religion is right? The congregation in the book of Hebrews really struggled with this question.

Their enthusiasm for Christianity started to dwindle, especially since life was becoming more and more difficult for them. They were Christians and yet things had not improved. This made them wonder whether God was really on their side.

Their neighbors, the Jews, were not a big help either. They wanted the Christians to become Jews again and argued that one can be sure that God is on the side of the Jews. Just look at the prophets, big leaders of God like Moses and Joshua, the high priest and all the altars and sacrifices.

Considering these examples of God's presence among the Jews, nobody could deny the fact that God was active among them. So, they argued, if Christians had doubts about God's power, they should rather become Jews again.

The author of the letter to the Hebrews says that to do this would be a big mistake. They should rather persevere with their eyes fixed on Jesus, whatever might happen. He believed there were good reasons for this perseverance in faith.

The author does not deny that God had been with the people of the Old Testament, but he goes on to tell them that things changed when Jesus, God's only Son, came to earth. In the past, God had spoken to the people of the Old Testament many times and in many ways through the prophets. However, in the last days, He had spoken to them through His Son, Jesus Christ (1:1-2). If one really wants to see which religion is the true one, one should compare what the Jews have with what believers have in Jesus.

The Jews argued that wherever there are angels, God is active, since the angels are His servants. But there is no comparison between Jesus and angels. The angels are servants of God, Jesus is His Son.

The same applies to their big leaders Moses and Joshua. They were special people, but they were still only God's servants who had the special task of leading God's people out of Egypt and into the Promised Land.

They are no match for Jesus, the Son of God, who leads the people of God into His new world. The choice is yours: who will you choose? The servant or the Son? The author says it most plainly when he explains that exchanging Christianity for something else would be like swapping diamonds for stones.

What about sin? The Jews had to receive forgiveness through sacrifices and intercession by the priests, especially the high priest.

What does Jesus offer? Well, Jesus died for our sins on our behalf – He made an atoning sacrifice that never needs to be repeated again. As God's Son, Jesus has direct access to His heavenly Father and can mediate on our behalf with the heavenly Judge. Direct representation in heaven – who could ask for more?

If you want to stay on the right path, you have to follow Jesus. Follow Him as your guide and leader through this life. It may sometimes prove difficult – just as the journey through the wilderness had proven difficult for the Israelites.

However, believers should persevere with their eyes fixed on Jesus. They must constantly draw inspiration from the believers that have gone before them. They persevered in difficult situations by standing firm in their faith, and they were victorious.

There are many reasons why one should remain faithful to Christ, even through hardship and suffering. If you keep your eyes on God, you will reach the Promised Land – of that you can be sure.

THE VALUE OF LIFE LIES IN BEING SOMEBODY TO SOMEONE

James and 1-3 John

> This is how we know what love is: Jesus Christ lay down His life for us. And we ought to lay down our lives for our brothers. If anyone has material possessions and sees his brother in need but has no pity on him, how can the love of God be in him?
>
> 1 JOHN 3:16-17

According to James, people who are searching for the value and meaning of life first have to gain the right perspective on life. Once you have the right perspective, you will be able to make the right choices.

He distinguishes between two ways of looking at life: firstly, looking at life through God's perspective (with God's wisdom) and secondly, looking at life from a human perspective (human wisdom). The perspective you choose will determine the way you handle life (3:13-18). The book of James lists many examples of how choosing God's perspective can enrich the value of a person's life.

James starts with a strange remark; he says that you should consider yourself fortunate if things go wrong with you (1:2-4). Humanly speaking this does not make any sense. How can experiencing difficulties bring you happiness? But from God's perspective things are different. Having difficulties can be a good thing – realizing your own limitations in a crisis may force you to seek real help and power elsewhere.

In this search you usually see God so much clearer because you need His helping hand even more. What could compare to feeling God's mighty arms around you when you're in need? Difficulties are like God's schooling plan; there you learn to re-assess your relationship with God.

People have a tendency of thinking that they can get along without God. This is a dangerous form of self-deception based on a very wrong outlook on life – the human perspective. We so often take our destiny into our own hands and plan our own lives: where we want to be, and what we want to do; even working out our finances in advance (4:13-17).

Don't misunderstand James' intention, God is not against meticulous planning, but God is not in favor of an attitude that assumes that humans are the masters of the universe.

There is another Master, and He is not a human. Humans may plan their own future but they cannot plan the route of the Angel of death. Humans have so little control over their own lives that they are not even sure whether they will still be alive in a few hours' time.

Therefore, it would be wise to include God in your planning; using His roadmap instead of your own. This way you will reach the destination God intends for you.

James also addressed the subject of money (1:9-11). Money shines, luring us into believing that true value and meaning in life is dependent on it. At least, this is what it looks like from a human perspective. From God's perspective, however, you see money for what it really is. It is a passing and fleeting thing, bringing temporary joy before vanishing.

If you sell your soul to money, you will lose your life to money. It is like a pretty flower that blossoms for a little while and then dies in the scorching rays of the sun. Material possessions do not last forever. Beautiful houses eventually collapse and expensive clothes will fade in the end.

The letters of John focus on love as the essence of a meaningful and sensible life. God is love and therefore His children should love one another. Since God first loved us, we are compelled to love one another (1 John 4).

But John also had other concerns – seeing

Jesus in the right perspective. We should worship Him for who He is and not make Him into something He isn't. He is God's divine Messiah, the Christ, who became human. To deny that He became a man, even though you worship Him as divine, makes you His opponent (1 John 2; 2 John).

In essence, if you only confess half the truth about Jesus, or don't believe in the whole truth of who He is, you actually believe nothing about Him (1 John 2:18-20; 4:1-2). You have to confess that Jesus is God's Messiah (sent King) who became human and died for our sins.

Having the right perspective on life will help you to live your life sensibly and meaningfully. Always approach life from God's perspective.

FOLLOW IN
JESUS' FOOTSTEPS

1, 2 Peter and Jude – Christianity
is not a popularity contest

> You know that it was not with perishable things such as silver or gold that you were redeemed from the empty way of life handed down to you from your forefathers, but with the precious blood of Christ, a lamb without blemish or defect.
>
> 1 PETER 1:18-19

Reality caught up with Peter's congregation. At first they were very excited about being Christians, but the non-believers started to treat them unfairly and harshly simply because they were Christian.

This made them wonder: is it worthwhile to remain Christians amidst such hardship and suffering?

Peter encouraged these believers to persevere. Listen to what he said, "Be self-controlled and alert. Your enemy the Devil prowls around like a roaring lion looking for someone to devour. Resist him, standing firm in the faith, because you know that your brothers throughout the world are undergoing the same kind of sufferings" (1 Pet. 5:8-9).

In these difficult times, they should not only realize who the enemy is, but also remember who they are. Believers are God's chosen people who have received His mercy; they are His children who belong to Him (1 Pet. 1:17-21; 2:9-10).

Jesus was also insulted but He never doubted Himself or God. Although the Devil might try to devour them by attacking and degrading them, God will keep them and protect them. They should trust in Him, come what may.

Peter explained the nature of the Christian life in this world in terms of a journey through a foreign country. That's why he refers to them as "strangers" in the world (1 Pet. 2:11).

They are God's people on their way to their Father in heaven, to collect their eternal inheritance (1 Pet. 1:3). Whatever may happen on this journey, it should not affect or upset them at all – it does not really concern them because this is not their land. They are only strangers here, people who are merely passing through.

If other people treat them badly or unfairly it will only be for a while, since their journey will take them to their "Homeland" in heaven where eternal glory awaits them. They should focus on that hope rather than on the sufferings they now endure.

Moreover, they should always remember that Jesus also suffered. The world did not like Him either. But He did not change His course, even in the face of death. This is the example that every Christian should follow.

But how should Christians behave on this journey, especially since they are just strangers in this world? Strangers can still carry out a message in this world, the message of Jesus.

By being who they are, God's people, they can introduce God's love, patience and Good News to this world (1 Pet. 3:8-12; 4:7-11). They should be holy as God is holy. They should leave impressions of Jesus with every person that they encounter on their journey. They should also "be Jesus" for one another through their forgiveness, love, help and support.

Both the congregations of Peter and Jude struggled with false teachers who confused them with all sorts of false theories. The advice of Peter and Jude to their congregations was short and simple: Leave such people alone and don't believe them or obey them.

Believers also had a lovely dream to live for, a dream that what God had promised will come true. They looked forward to the time when the Lord would return to lead them to their heavenly destination.

There were moments when they wondered what was keeping the Lord from returning.

Unbelievers even mocked them by saying it would never happen.

What these mockers did not realize was that God does not work according to the time-table of this world. A thousand years is like one day for God (2 Pet. 3).

He will return – when the time is right. Instead of trying to set His watch for Him, Christians should rather wait patiently. What is certain, is that He will return.

In the meantime, those who do not believe should make use of their time of grace to repent and turn to God.

MAKE SURE YOU ARE ON THE SIDE OF THE RIGHT KING

Revelation shows you how to persevere and endure

I heard a loud voice from the throne saying, "Now the dwelling of God is with men, and He will live with them. They will be His people, and God Himself will be with them and be their God. He will wipe every tear from their eyes. There will be no more death or mourning or crying or pain, for the old order of things has passed away."

REVELATION 21:3-4

If you could have peeped over the shoulder of God while He was planning the history of the universe, what would you have seen?

John, the author of Revelation, knows, because God revealed it to him. God invited him to heaven and showed him the flow of the history of this world (1:1-5; 4:1). What did he see?

The history of the world is like a war; it is a battle between good and evil. As in any war, there are armies – a good one and an evil one, each with its own leader. John was invited to visit both armies.

John first visited the good army, God's army. What an experience that was! As he entered heaven, the door opened into the throne room of the King, the Ruler of the universe!

The atmosphere was electrifying, filled with holiness, faithfulness and immeasurable power. Everybody worshiped the King on His throne and sang, "Holy, Holy, Holy is the Lord God Almighty" (4).

Then John saw Jesus. Jesus had already conquered the Devil. Jesus actually died so that every believer could live – and not just live, but live eternally. Jesus conquered death.

That is why He holds the keys of death and life in His hands (1). As the Rider on the white horse, He will lead the army of heaven in its final assault to destroy the Devil forever (19).

God's people, a whole army of them, also caught John's eye (7). Jesus saved all of them from sin so that they could be God's children. They are overflowing with praise and worship to God. Moreover, nothing could stop them from spreading the Good News of God. Their weapons were not swords and spears, but the gospel of salvation through Jesus.

Then John turned to the army of the Devil and this proved to be a very different experience. God's judgment was hanging over them like the stench of death. They were the losers and they knew it. Their commander, the Devil, was making one final attempt to hurt God's children. He was using every cunning tactic he could muster to mislead people into worshiping him instead of God (12-15).

Yet God will not tolerate evil behavior forever. A time will come when the King of the universe will say, "Enough is enough." Then the Rider on the white horse will finally destroy the Devil, and with him, every knee that will not bow before Jesus (20). Nobody will escape God's final judgment.

A wonderful future awaits God's people. God Himself will live among His people. In the new city, Jerusalem, He will dry all their tears, and illness, death and hate will not be a part of their lives any longer.

Although we cannot change the future, it helps to know what it is going to be like. We need to make sure that we are on the side of the King, and that we stay there!

Discover God's

Plan for Your Life

10 LIFE-CHANGING TRUTHS

1. Discover God – for the first time and once again

How can we get to know God?

The Bible tells us of a God who has been there since the very beginning. He is the One who made everything. God's footprints lie between our everyday experiences. It is in being sensitive to these ordinary things that we hear His voice. The Bible tells us all about this extraordinary God who is in the midst of people's ordinary lives.

We especially learn about God as the God of His people. God made an agreement with Abraham and his family – He would be their God if they would be His people, people completely devoted to Him, listening to what He tells them to do in order to live in peace, happiness, and harmony (all of these instructions were recorded in the Law).

It is here, among His people, entwined in their history, that we get to meet God. He is not removed from them. No, He protects them, leads them, cares for them, is loving and faithful towards them. What's even more amazing is that He has loving patience with them even when they start to get rebellious. God forgave them again and again. However, God's patience can also come to an end, and then His love is expressed in the form of punishment. Especially when no other way seems effective in convincing the people to listen to God.

It is impossible to sum up who God is in one sentence. Throughout the history recorded in the Bible, we see so many rich and varied facets of God's character and nature.

Yet some of God's characteristics shine through more brightly than others: like the fact that God is loving, gracious and faithful.

He never left His people even when they turned away from Him. The disobedience of His people eventually led to their exile in Babylon. As we've already seen, God's patience has some boundaries.

But in His great mercy God brought His people out of exile after some time had passed. He is, after all, the God to whom all power and might belongs, and therefore, also the future. Through His prophets, God promised that He would be with His people in a special, but new way.

This promise came true ... in Jesus. Through Jesus, God broke the barrier between heaven and earth. For the first time, people could see and hear the invisible God! Whoever looked at Jesus could see God at work and hear His loving heart beat. Jesus came to set people free from their sin, because whoever believes in Him will get God's promised gift of eternal life. The miracles that Jesus performed, especially His resurrection from the dead, showed clearly that God had sent Him.

Who other than God could possibly break the gates of death? His wonderful teaching about a love that makes God happy, brought something of God's paradise to earth. God's people were now back on the journey with Him – a journey to an everlasting future with God.

When Jesus returned to His Father He left His Holy Spirit with us and He lives in each person that has accepted the Good News of God. God's Spirit made His home in ordinary people like you and me; He made us His holy temples.

God's power enters the world every day through the faithful actions and joy-filled smiles of ordinary believers. God is no longer removed and distant, He is near, as near as the closest child of God is to you.

This is how we learn about God, not through abstract theories, but through real experience. We read about God's wonder on every page of the Bible. God is not a theory, He lives among us, and is a part of the big things and the small things that happen every day.

2. Discover ... yourself

Who are you? This is a question that could keep you busy for a very long time! Philosophers, theologians, psychologists and teachers have all tried to explain who and what a human is. What do you think?

Let's hear what God has to say about this. After all, God created people, so He ought to know the answer best. If God were to write an instruction manual, what do you think He would write in it?

Well, it would say that God made humans good, and He intended them to live in harmony with Him, faithfully serving Him in His paradise. In the "Manual" we find that people are at their happiest when they live close to God.

Yes, when God's love becomes your love, when His strength becomes your strength, when His friendliness becomes your friendliness, then you are truly the person God intended you to be. If you live close to God, enjoy a real living friendship with Him, and serve Him from the depths of your heart, then you're living just as the "Manual" says you ought to.

God made people good, but unfortunately people didn't stay good for long. This is not because God made a bad "product", but because the "product" wanted to be better than the Producer. God made humans very special, in fact God made us in His own image. He gave humans free will in order to make their own decisions. God did not want to force people to serve Him. God wanted people to choose to honor Him out of their own free will. Why? Simply because it is wonderful to serve someone you love.

But people wanted to be their own boss, in fact they wanted to play God, and in this selfishness, the good and close relationship with God, was broken. People wanted to sort everything out for themselves, without God's help.

This can only mean one thing: we must now turn to the page in the "Manual" that tells us what to do when the "product" breaks. There we read that we mustn't try to fix ourselves. We are so caught up in our own concerns that we would just make things worse.

Through our desire for independence, instead of trusting God to help us, we'll only draw away from Him as we try to fix ourselves. The "Manual" shows us a better way – we can only become whole again in the hands of the One who made us in the first place. With Him alone can we become the people whom He intended us to be … people who live with, and for, God.

Let's ask the question again: "Who are you?" Do you live according to God's Manual? If you're not living according to the "Manual", it's not because you've been created that way, but because you've chosen to live that way. It is how you choose to live. It's your choice.

Of course you also have the freedom to choose to live according to the "Manual" … that is, to live close to God, to draw from His strength, to enjoy His love, to faithfully serve Him, and to choose to live for Him each and every day.

So, who are you? and what do you choose?

3. Discover forgiveness that gives you a chance to start over again

Every now and then we all need a chance to start over again. Sometimes things just go wrong. But God also walks with us on this journey. God is not just there for the winners. He is there for those who feel that they can't go on anymore, for those who feel that life has given them one blow too many.

Of course sin breaks God's heart, but it doesn't harden it; certainly not when we place our heartache and mistakes into His loving hands. When we do this He is quick to forgive and give us a chance to start over again. Indeed, forgiveness is that wonderful moment when God wraps His hand more firmly around us because He feels our searching hand in His.

Forgiveness … it's God's special medicine for people who make mistakes. If it weren't for Adam and Eve, or Paul and Peter, the gulf between God and us would have been too great to overcome. Forgiveness is godly. It fixes relationships and it builds bridges so that people can start over with God.

But how does it work? True faith, sometimes called true religion, has to do with our relationship with God and our faithful service to Him. So, it is not about what we do, but about who we *are*. We *are* children of God, people who live close to Him.

We must do our best to keep that relationship right and healthy, because if our relationship with God is healthy, then we will do what is right. Not only will we do what is right, we will also *want* to do what is right.

John (1 John 1:6-10) tells us very clearly how God's medicine for a healthy relationship with Him works. If we make a mistake, we need to fix it, because our relationship with God will suffer because of that mistake. So, we need to fix our relationship with God right away. Some people call this medicine *confession of sin.*

The first sip of medicine is intended to help you admit your wrongdoing. You have to admit that you did wrong, and also admit that what you did was wrong. We all know how difficult it can be, for example, to apologize to someone that we fought with. But we know that it is the right thing to do.

The second sip of medicine is to tell God

that you're sorry and that you will try to never do what you did again. In effect you're saying to God that you don't want to make that mistake again. It is perhaps the most difficult part of the recovery process … to let go of bad behaviors that have become a habit, like a swear word every now and then, or gossip that just seems to slip out of your mouth. You just have to say goodbye to such behavior for the sake of your relationship with God.

The third sip of medicine that helps in your recovery, is to give your heart to God again. You have to tell God that you belong to Him and no one else. To sit in His lap again and feel His arms around you while you put your arms around Him, and to know you don't want to serve anyone but Him.

True faith is to discover God and to know that you are always welcome to sit on His lap because He has forgiven you, and still forgives you. Whenever you make a mistake you can start over, because He is a God of forgiveness and grace.

4. Discover the true meaning of life

God has given you a gift that no one can ever take from you: the gift of life. God placed the gift of this life in your hands and said, "Live it." This life is your responsibility, and no one else's. You'd better use it well!

The big question is: What are you doing with your gift from God? How are you living your life? Have you discovered the purpose of it yet? Would you be able to look back on your life at its end and say that it was worth it?

Of course you can choose to live your life in many ways, but of one thing you must be sure, not everything you dedicate your life to is worthwhile. Well, what is worth it? In the wisdom books of the Bible (like Ecclesiastes, Job, Proverbs and James) we read what God thinks is worthwhile.

If you don't have a goal for your life, something that you're aiming at, then your life will be like a bobbing boat on the sea. You are moving, but you're not sure where you're heading and why you're heading in that direction.

We could, for instance, dedicate our lives to material things, like so many people choose to do these days. With every decision we make we first ask the question, what is this going to cost? Am I going to get anything out of it? Even when we choose our friends, we first check to see where they live and what kind of car they drive.

Well, as life has shown again and again, the most expensive clothes get dirty and tear, even expensive cars rust and break down, and money runs out. The Bible warns us that these things are not permanent. Why on earth would you want to devote your life to something that will just pass away? Is it really worth it?

Another possibility is to live for something less visible, like status and the recognition of others. This is a very difficult road to walk, because when things start to go wrong the very people you tried to impress will turn their backs on you before you know it! In any case, do you really think that when you no longer have that important position, that anyone will remember you after you have cleared out your office?

The question is: Do you want to put all of your time, energy, and talent, into something that can disappear instantly? Is it worth sacrificing your family, your spouse, your children, yourself, simply so that a few people can applaud you? You see, you can devote your life to many things, but you must always ask yourself if it is worthwhile.

You can also discover a life that is truly worthwhile – a life with God. This is not a life that will ever end. It is permanent. Its blessing and joy will last forever. As Ecclesiastes tells us, this is a life that you can live to the full and enjoy forever. God wants us to enjoy every moment of life, He wants us to go through life with a song in our hearts.

Our actions should be filled with joy, but it should always have one goal: to remain faithful and close to God. You don't have to sit in church night and day to achieve this life.

No, God's church is His Creation. In the wonder of His Creation you can enjoy everything that He created to the full, but always remember to do it in a way that will please God. If God is satisfied with what you're doing then you know you're on the right road. Then you're living your life as God planned for you.

We have to have an anchor or a purpose for our lives; it could be God, or we could choose something else. You can work out what your anchor in life is by taking an honest look at what you spend most of your time and energy doing. Make sure you choose wisely!

5. Discover the people around you in love

We can't make it without other people. God created us to be in relationships with others.

It's interesting to see that in just about every instance where the Bible talks about true religion, it deals with how we should behave towards other people. James, for example, says that true faith is to help others who are in need (James 1-2).

Then according to John, Jesus' beloved disciple, the most important lesson that Jesus taught was to wash one another's feet (John 13). Of course this is just another way of saying that we need to care for the people around us. We should never think that we are too important or too busy to kneel next to someone and help them, no matter how humble the task.

Knowing and loving God allows one to see other people from a completely different perspective. It allows one to see that it is not really important what clothes a person wears, but rather who that person is.

A very creative and gifted person made those lovely clothes, but that can never compare to the miracle that God has performed in creating the person who wears the clothes!

So, to love God means to love God's Creation, which means we have to look beyond the outward appearance of a person, and look toward the real person within.

It's there, between ordinary people, that your true faith is revealed – service to God. Indeed, the world is God's holy temple; God can be honored and served in the poorest home, or on the side of the busiest street.

In fact, wherever there are people, God can be glorified. True faith takes shape next to and in front of other people. It is the *love* that you share with others that allows true faith to increase. True love is meant to be shared among people – love is the loyal binding factor and support that brings people together. It has to do with an attitude of always wanting to do your best for others.

True love never stays just words. Love truly

becomes love when it is expressed in what we do (we can read all about this in 1 Cor. 13 or Gal. 5). Love takes shape in practical things, such as not keeping a record of the wrongs that others have done against you. Why on earth would you want to remember that? Are you keeping it so that you can get back at them? Surely true love cannot allow this to happen!

Practically, love means not being jealous or impatient with others. Jealousy robs people of things, because you rather want it all for yourself. Yet the Lord created each one of us uniquely with our own special gifts and talents.

If your jealousy tries to stop someone else from being what the Lord created him or her to be, surely that cannot be true love? Rather, make peace with who you are, and then you can grow to become who God has created you to be.

Love smiles. It is friendly, but it is not a shallow or false friendliness. It doesn't wear a mask, pretending to smile, yet hiding hate behind it. True friendliness means that people are not afraid to be with you, that they feel secure and comfortable enough to pour out their hearts in your presence.

They know that what they say is safe with you, because they can feel your trustworthiness and friendliness shielding and protecting them. And so we can go on … love never wants to hurt anyone, but it wants to heal those who hurt.

True love lets you see other people as God sees them, His beautiful Creation. You need to act towards others as if it is God Himself who is standing in front of you. And that can only be done in love.

6. Discover God's strength in your life

One specific part of the biblical message makes a person wonder: If Christians are children of God, the King and Creator of the world, why do things sometimes go so wrong for them?

Just look at how some people suffer. And then the question: "Surely their Father, who is almighty and perfectly good, could help them out of every situation and struggle?" People start to wonder, especially when things start going wrong with them: "Where is God? Has He forgotten about me?"

Sometimes we forget too easily that we're not in heaven yet. God promised He would dry away our tears and heal all our diseases. But we still have to wait for Jesus to return for us; and that has not happened yet.

Until then evil is still all around us, and that means that we will experience suffering and hardship. The Evil One's intention with God's people is not friendly or innocent. No, quite the opposite, the Evil One's plan is to try and hurt God's people. This is the reality of the world in which we live.

But what is God's promise in a world like this? God never promised that He would change every situation so that we would never have any struggles. God also never said that because He loves us we would be safe from the hardships of life (see Rom. 8:31 onwards). If this was true then it would mean that God didn't love Paul, Peter, or even Jesus, because all of them faced trouble and strife.

No, what God did promise us is that He would give us the strength to face our difficulties. He's not going to change the situation, but He is going to change us so that we remain strong and steadfast in any situation. Paul himself said it so well, "I can do everything through Him who gives me strength" (Phil. 4:13).

Just like electrical power flows through wires, God's power flows through relationships. The power you get from someone close to you. You get your strength from His strength. That's why, for example, a little child is not afraid to be in the dark as long as his or her mother is there. The mother's strength becomes the child's strength.

It is the same with God's strength. You know that He is there with you, even when you are facing your darkest moments. It is by recognizing God's presence, trusting that He is there with you, holding you and protecting you, that you get the strength to carry on.

No matter how difficult things are, if you hold on to the reality that God is there with you, you won't be crushed. Your heart will be filled with courage. After all, is there anything in this world that can compare to God's power, love, and grace? It was for this very reason that Paul asked, "Who or what could ever separate us from the love of God?" There is nothing.

So it all boils down to having the right perspective on life's challenges. No matter what's on the line, there can be nothing more precious than the knowledge of God's powerful presence strengthening you to face life. Remember, your current circumstances and your eternal life are all safe in the palm of God's mighty hand.

God doesn't necessarily change situations (although, He sometimes does), but He changes people to be able to face any situation. It is in this knowledge that every Christian can have true victory. No matter how tough life may be, the power of God can keep them standing strong.

7. Discover God's roadmap for your life

People have rights, human rights. This seems to be the dominant philosophy of our time. Of course one of the central elements of this philosophy is that it allows every person the freedom to make their own decisions. Freedom of speech is another fundamental right.

The result is that if anyone tries to dictate to someone else, they've committed a deadly sin. Moreover, human rights also state that we're all equal, so how could one person say that they know better, or more, than another? Authority is certainly no longer a very popular word!

This is precisely where our faith clashes with the philosophy of the day. With human rights, people are placed at the center. With religion, God is at the center. If a person decides that God must occupy that spot in his life, he gives up the right to decide what's right and what's wrong. That becomes God's choice.

The only sensible thing to do is to listen to God. Of course whether the world accepts it or not, God ultimately has all authority to tell people what He expects of them. God doesn't have to listen to what people think, as if God was merely one of us; people have to listen to God.

In this age of self-determination, people find that difficult to do.

Fortunately, what God wants and what people want are not all that far removed from one another. After all, God did create us, and for that reason God wants us to be happy. Human rights ultimately wants the same thing –

that things should go well with people and that they should be happy. Both talk about love, peace and contentment. However, what differs radically, is the route that each one maps out to reach that joy and peace.

Jesus gave us God's roadmap to peace and contentment. It is for that reason that Jesus is known as "the Way, the Truth, and the Life" (John 14:6). So, if anyone is searching for the truth that will lead him or her to true life, they will have to look to Him to find it. That means that people will not be able to discover and fabricate their own truth. Real truth is something that we can only get from Jesus.

What does this roadmap from God look like? Well, Jesus followed this map. It is a route of loving other people. A road filled with grace, forgiveness, patience and goodness. Of course we read the same things about this map in the Law of God where God instructed His people not to murder and steal. That is the road that God wants us to take.

However, this road has boundaries. True love can never rejoice over anything that does not bring God happiness, no matter how much people want it. True love always seeks to please God first. So, if a person does something that displeases God, the road of love cannot simply help that person along.

True love draws the line at sin. That doesn't mean that love ends at the line, or turns away from it. No, it crosses the line with one goal in mind, to bring the person who sinned back to the right side of the road.

It is our responsibility to show a person where he has gone wrong and to do everything in our power to help him to get back on the right road again – even if it may mean some hard words are spoken. However, all the difficult attempts and hard words must be wrapped in love so that this love will get the person on God's side of the road again.

God doesn't let His children wander around aimlessly without a roadmap to guide them. Take God's map with you on your life's journey. It will not only help you to reach the right destination, but you'll reach it with joy.

8. Discover that you can make a difference

Christians tend to underestimate themselves. They often wonder whether they can mean anything to God. More often than not we walk around with a guilty conscience because we think our mistakes just disappoint God. We get so caught up in what we've done wrong that we forget to concentrate on doing what is good and right.

Let's take a look at what God thinks about us. Does God simply see us as a bunch of failures that don't mean much to Him? Or who do you think God would place in His "photo album" of heroes? We don't have to wonder about that, because the Bible tells us whom God put into His photo album.

In one of the photos we'll see a little old lady who could only put a few cents into the collection plate, yet it was all that she had (Luke 21:4). Yes, she gave everything she had. Amongst all the people that were there that day Jesus noticed her, and gave her a special place in His book of heroes. God doesn't look at how thick your purse is, He looks at your heart.

There's another photo of a little boy who brought five little loaves of bread and two fish to Jesus and His disciples when they needed food to feed thousands of people (John 6). He took what he had and he placed it in the Lord's hands and with that the Lord fed thousands. What a miracle! Trust me, God doesn't want to look at how good we are, He rather wants to see what He can do through us.

Then we see the picture of the little slave girl in a foreign land. She saw how sick the owner of the house was and that no doctor could cure him. So she told him about her God who could help, knowing full well that if her sick master made the effort to go to a foreign land and was not healed there, she would pay for it with her life. Still, that didn't stop her from doing what she had to do, because she trusted in God. God didn't disappoint her, because she didn't disappoint God.

A few cents, five loaves and two small fish, a shy testimony of God's power from a slave girl ... those are the kinds of things you'll find in God's photo album. This shows how important the little things are to God. God never asks for more than we can give. No, He simply asks for what we have. When we live generously, God gives us a special place in His photo album of heroes.

God doesn't want you to wage wars on His behalf, or cross oceans and deserts before He'll notice you. God simply wants you to be yourself, just where you are now. Give God what you have, whether it's a few cents, or just two little fish.

Don't think too little of yourself as a Christian. God *can* use you, and wants to use you in mighty ways! You don't have to be a pastor or a priest to be used by God. Just be who God created you to be, and walk faithfully and closely with God.

Put your talents – whether they are many or few – in the hands of the Lord so that He can do with them what He wants.

You'll be astounded at what God can do with your talents to enrich and change the lives of others. That's the mystery of how God works.

9. Discover God's presence through His Spirit

Christians are Jesus-people – they should be like Jesus. They have to follow in Jesus' footsteps and do what Jesus did, not only in their relationship with God, but also in their relationships with other people.

Let's be honest, that's not always easy. Christians are just ordinary people after all, and no one knows that better than the Lord.

It is for this very reason that God gave us a Special Helper – Someone who can help us up when we fall, who guides us when we're not sure which road to take, Someone who can strengthen us when we think our strength is gone. This helper is God's own Spirit.

So what does the Spirit do? Well, the Holy Spirit works in many marvelous ways in the lives of ordinary believers. The Spirit doesn't only help us in our spiritual lives, He also helps us in our everyday, ordinary lives. Let's have a brief peek at the items that are listed on the Spirit's daily to-do list:

 † The Spirit gives new life. It is through His power that the believer is born again (John 3). It is the Spirit who opens our eyes to see God and know that He is there with us. It is the Spirit who helps us to see the spiritual world of God and appreciate it. Without the Spirit you would be like a blind person

in a dark room – you simply would not see and experience anything about God.

† It is also the work of the Spirit that helps the believer to "grow up" as a good child in God's family. Children have to learn how to behave properly, and the Spirit teaches us how to do this.

So, whoever obediently and diligently follows the leading of the Holy Spirit will begin to bear the fruit of the Spirit, for example, love, kindness, patience, and all those things that we read about in Galatians 5. We also don't have to wonder about how to deal with difficult situations because the answer is just a prayer away – we simply need to ask the Spirit and He will lead us in the truth (John 14-15).

† The Spirit is also there to help us when we are not sure what to say to our heavenly Father. The Spirit helps us by taking those thoughts and feelings that lie deep within our hearts, thoughts that we cannot even put into words, and whispers them in the ear of God (Rom. 8).

† The Spirit is also like a pharmacist for the congregation. If He sees that the congregation is struggling, or is "sick" in some way, He ensures that the right medicine is provided.

We read in a few places in the Bible about the gifts that the Spirit gives to the congregation to build it up and make it strong (1 Cor. 13, Rom. 12). It is the Spirit that holds our hand when it feels like it is going to slip out of God's hand; the Spirit brings us healing when we feel spiritually sick.

† When someone has to testify for the Lord but his knees are buckling with fear, it is the Spirit who comes to his aid. No one can silence Him. It is He that speaks through us. And when we walk away from people, it is the Spirit who stays behind to work in their hearts and minds.

So believers have nothing to fear because God is with them through His Spirit. That means that Christians are not only Jesus-people, they are also Spirit-people! Christians should live each day in a faithful and intimate relationship with the Spirit. It is only in this way that they will be able to hear Him clearly and follow Him faithfully.

This intimate relationship is the fountain of strength in the life of the believer. Christians are never alone; they have the Spirit of God!

10. Discover the meaning of everything

If Christians ever wonder who they really are, they'll see Jesus, who rose from the dead, standing in front of them like a lighthouse in the darkness.

The message is loud and clear: There is life after death! If this wasn't so, Jesus would never have been able to rise from the dead and carry on living. What happens to us in this life is certainly not the end. No, it is merely part of our beginning with God.

For this reason we could speak about Christians as "future-people", because we have a future with God. We are not blinded by what happens to us in this lifetime, we look forward to what will come in the next life – the eternal life. Death is not the end, it is merely a doorway to a new beginning.

Christians have so much to look forward to. At some stage in the future, Jesus promised, He will return to fetch His own people so that they can spend eternity with God. Won't that be a celebration. To be one great big family living with God in His holiness!

The book of Revelation tries to describe this scene. We read that it will be like living in the most incredibly wealthy, magnificent city. A city with streets of gold. A place where there is an abundance of food, health, friendship and joy.

All the terrible things that demoralize us in this world, like abuse, lies, hurt, sickness and corruption, will not exist in heaven. God will make sure of that. He will dry all our tears and heal all our diseases, He promises to take away all our pain. With Him there will be nothing but joy and peace.

Even this incredible description of heaven is not complete … what will it really feel like to be there? What will we do when we're there? This description of the city of gold and jewels is, after all, only a poor human attempt at describing how wonderful it will be.

If you were a person who was hungry and didn't have any money for food, or if you were very sick, then imagine how wonderful this promise sounds. What we need to do is imagine the most incredible and marvelous things, and then multiply them by thousands.

Only then will we begin to catch a glimpse of how wonderful it will be in heaven. To be honest, not even our wildest dreams can come close to what it will really be like.

But let's look at an illustration that may just be able to help us picture what it could be like. A baby who is still in his mother's womb thinks that life is just perfect. He has everything that he needs, food, warmth, the closeness of his mother and a host of other things that keep him content. And then he is born. He sees the blue sky and the green mountains. He learns that it is far better to lie in your mother's arms, and he learns what love truly means.

He suddenly learns that there is so much more to the world than he could ever know or imagine. It is a completely different world. In the same way we can hardly imagine what it is going to be like to live with God.

In this world we are a bit like that baby in his mother's womb. We haven't yet realized what it is like in God's world. All that we know is what God promises us – that it is going to be wonderful.

Christians know that their true destination is not here on earth. For that reason they ought not to lay their anchors too deeply in this world, or use up all their energy to build themselves little kingdoms on earth.

Their kingdom lies with the King of kings, the God of the whole universe. Therefore we can say that they're "future-people". They live with the expectation of what is to come. And the good news is that the best is yet to come!

WISDOM FROM THE WORD

Husbands, in the same way be considerate as you live with your wives, and treat them with respect as the weaker partner and as heirs with you of the gracious gift of life.

1 PETER 3:7

Husbands, love your wives. Each one of you also must love his wife as he loves himself.

EPHESIANS 5:25, 33

Fathers, do not exasperate your children; instead, bring them up in the training and instruction of the Lord.

EPHESIANS 6:4

Fathers, do not embitter your children, or they will become discouraged.

COLOSSIANS 3:21

He must manage his own family well and see that his children obey him with proper respect.

1 TIMOTHY 3:4

Teach the older men to be temperate, worthy of respect, self-controlled, and sound in faith, in love and in endurance.

TITUS 2:2

Brothers ... Let your "Yes" be yes, and your "No," no.

JAMES 5:12

So then, brothers, stand firm and hold to the teachings we passed on to you.

2 THESSALONIANS 2:15

My son, do not despise the LORD's discipline and do not resent His rebuke, because the LORD disciplines those he loves, as a father the son he delights in.

PROVERBS 3:11-12

The righteous man leads a blameless life; blessed are his children after him.

PROVERBS 20:7

Faith is being sure of what we hope for and certain of what we do not see.

HEBREWS 11:1

Blessed is the man who makes the LORD his trust.

PSALM 40:4

READ THROUGH THE BIBLE IN ONE YEAR

January

1	Genesis 1-2	Psalm 1	Matthew 1-2
2	Genesis 3-4	Psalm 2	Matthew 3-4
3	Genesis 5-7	Psalm 3	Matthew 5
4	Genesis 8-9	Psalm 4	Matthew 6-7
5	Genesis 10-11	Psalm 5	Matthew 8-9
6	Genesis 12-13	Psalm 6	Matthew 10-11
7	Genesis 14-15	Psalm 7	Matthew 12
8	Genesis 16-17	Psalm 8	Matthew 13
9	Genesis 18-19	Psalm 9	Matthew 14-15
10	Genesis 20-21	Psalm 10	Matthew 16-17
11	Genesis 22-23	Psalm 11	Matthew 18
12	Genesis 24	Psalm 12	Matthew 19-20
13	Genesis 25-26	Psalm 13	Matthew 21
14	Genesis 27-28	Psalm 14	Matthew 22
15	Genesis 29-30	Psalm 15	Matthew 23
16	Genesis 31-32	Psalm 16	Matthew 24
17	Genesis 33-34	Psalm 17	Matthew 25
18	Genesis 35-36	Psalm 18	Matthew 26
19	Genesis 37-38	Psalm 19	Matthew 27
20	Genesis 39-40	Psalm 20	Matthew 28
21	Genesis 41-42	Psalm 21	Mark 1
22	Genesis 43-44	Psalm 22	Mark 2
23	Genesis 45-46	Psalm 23	Mark 3
24	Genesis 47-48	Psalm 24	Mark 4
25	Genesis 49-50	Psalm 25	Mark 5
26	Exodus 1-2	Psalm 26	Mark 6
27	Exodus 3-4	Psalm 27	Mark 7
28	Exodus 5-6	Psalm 28	Mark 8
29	Exodus 7-8	Psalm 29	Mark 9
30	Exodus 9-10	Psalm 30	Mark 10
31	Exodus 11-12	Psalm 31	Mark 11

February

1	Exodus 13-14	Psalm 32	Mark 12
2	Exodus 15-16	Psalm 33	Mark 13
3	Exodus 17-18	Psalm 34	Mark 14
4	Exodus 19-20	Psalm 35	Mark 15
5	Exodus 21-22	Psalm 36	Mark 16
6	Exodus 23-24	Psalm 37	Luke 1
7	Exodus 25-26	Psalm 38	Luke 2
8	Exodus 27-28	Psalm 39	Luke 3
9	Exodus 29-30	Psalm 40	Luke 4
10	Exodus 31-32	Psalm 41	Luke 5
11	Exodus 33-34	Psalm 42	Luke 6
12	Exodus 35-36	Psalm 43	Luke 7
13	Exodus 37-38	Psalm 44	Luke 8
14	Exodus 39-40	Psalm 45	Luke 9
15	Leviticus 1-2	Psalm 46	Luke 10
16	Leviticus 3-4	Psalm 47	Luke 11
17	Leviticus 5-6	Psalm 48	Luke 12
18	Leviticus 7-8	Psalm 49	Luke 13
19	Leviticus 9-10	Psalm 50	Luke 14
20	Leviticus 11-12	Psalm 51	Luke 15
21	Leviticus 13	Psalm 52	Luke 16
22	Leviticus 14	Psalm 53	Luke 17
23	Leviticus 15-16	Psalm 54	Luke 18
24	Leviticus 17-18	Psalm 55	Luke 19
25	Leviticus 19-20	Psalm 56	Luke 20
26	Leviticus 21-22	Psalm 57	Luke 21
27	Leviticus 23-24	Psalm 58	Luke 22
28	Leviticus 25	Psalm 59	Luke 23

March

1	Leviticus 26-27	Psalm 60	Luke 24
2	Numbers 1-2	Psalm 61	John 1
3	Numbers 3-4	Psalm 62	John 2-3
4	Numbers 5-6	Psalm 63	John 4
5	Numbers 7	Psalm 64	John 5
6	Numbers 8-9	Psalm 65	John 6
7	Numbers 10-11	Psalm 66	John 7
8	Numbers 12-13	Psalm 67	John 8
9	Numbers 14-15	Psalm 68	John 9
10	Numbers 16	Psalm 69	John 10
11	Numbers 17-18	Psalm 70	John 11
12	Numbers 19-20	Psalm 71	John 12
13	Numbers 21-22	Psalm 72	John 13
14	Numbers 23-24	Psalm 73	John 14-15
15	Numbers 25-26	Psalm 74	John 16
16	Numbers 27-28	Psalm 75	John 17
17	Numbers 29-30	Psalm 76	John 18
18	Numbers 31-32	Psalm 77	John 19
19	Numbers 33-34	Psalm 78	John 20
20	Numbers 35-36	Psalm 79	John 21
21	Deuteronomy 1-2	Psalm 80	Acts 1
22	Deuteronomy 3-4	Psalm 81	Acts 2
23	Deuteronomy 5-6	Psalm 82	Acts 3-4
24	Deuteronomy 7-8	Psalm 83	Acts 5-6
25	Deuteronomy 9-10	Psalm 84	Acts 7
26	Deuteronomy 11-12	Psalm 85	Acts 8
27	Deuteronomy 13-14	Psalm 86	Acts 9
28	Deuteronomy 15-16	Psalm 87	Acts 10
29	Deuteronomy 17-18	Psalm 88	Acts 11-12
30	Deuteronomy 19-20	Psalm 89	Acts 13
31	Deuteronomy 21-22	Psalm 90	Acts 14

April

1	Deuteronomy 23-24	Psalm 91	Acts 15
2	Deuteronomy 25-27	Psalm 92	Acts 16
3	Deuteronomy 28-29	Psalm 93	Acts 17
4	Deuteronomy 30-31	Psalm 94	Acts 18
5	Deuteronomy 32	Psalm 95	Acts 19
6	Deuteronomy 33-34	Psalm 96	Acts 20
7	Joshua 1-2	Psalm 97	Acts 21
8	Joshua 3-4	Psalm 98	Acts 22
9	Joshua 5-6	Psalm 99	Acts 23
10	Joshua 7-8	Psalm 100	Acts 24-25
11	Joshua 9-10	Psalm 101	Acts 26
12	Joshua 11-12	Psalm 102	Acts 27
13	Joshua 13-14	Psalm 103	Acts 28
14	Joshua 15-16	Psalm 104	Romans 1-2
15	Joshua 17-18	Psalm 105	Romans 3-4
16	Joshua 19-20	Psalm 106	Romans 5-6
17	Joshua 21-22	Psalm 107	Romans 7-8
18	Joshua 23-24	Psalm 108	Romans 9-10
19	Judges 1-2	Psalm 109	Romans 11-12
20	Judges 3-4	Psalm 110	Romans 13-14
21	Judges 5-6	Psalm 111	Romans 15-16
22	Judges 7-8	Psalm 112	1 Corinthians 1-2
23	Judges 9	Psalm 113	1 Corinthians 3-4
24	Judges 10-11	Psalm 114	1 Corinthians 5-6
25	Judges 12-13	Psalm 115	1 Corinthians 7
26	Judges 14-15	Psalm 116	1 Corinthians 8-9
27	Judges 16-17	Psalm 117	1 Corinthians 10
28	Judges 18-19	Psalm 118	1 Corinthians 11
29	Judges 20-21	Psalm 119:1-88	1 Corinthians 12
30	Ruth 1-4	Psalm 119:89-176	1 Corinthians 13

May

1	1 Samuel 1-2	Psalm 120	1 Corinthians 14
2	1 Samuel 3-4	Psalm 121	1 Corinthians 15
3	1 Samuel 5-6	Psalm 122	1 Corinthians 16
4	1 Samuel 7-8	Psalm 123	2 Corinthians 1
5	1 Samuel 9-10	Psalm 124	2 Corinthians 2-3
6	1 Samuel 11-12	Psalm 125	2 Corinthians 4-5
7	1 Samuel 13-14	Psalm 126	2 Corinthians 6-7
8	1 Samuel 15-16	Psalm 127	2 Corinthians 8
9	1 Samuel 17	Psalm 128	2 Corinthians 9-10
10	1 Samuel 18-19	Psalm 129	2 Corinthians 11
11	1 Samuel 20-21	Psalm 130	2 Corinthians 12
12	1 Samuel 22-23	Psalm 131	2 Corinthians 13
13	1 Samuel 24-25	Psalm 132	Galatians 1-2
14	1 Samuel 26-27	Psalm 133	Galatians 3-4
15	1 Samuel 28-29	Psalm 134	Galatians 5-6
16	1 Samuel 30-31	Psalm 135	Ephesians 1-2
17	2 Samuel 1-2	Psalm 136	Ephesians 3-4
18	2 Samuel 3-4	Psalm 137	Ephesians 5-6
19	2 Samuel 5-6	Psalm 138	Philippians 1-2
20	2 Samuel 7-8	Psalm 139	Philippians 3-4
21	2 Samuel 9-10	Psalm 140	Colossians 1-2
22	2 Samuel 11-12	Psalm 141	Colossians 3-4
23	2 Samuel 13-14	Psalm 142	1 Thessalonians 1-2
24	2 Samuel 15-16	Psalm 143	1 Thessalonians 3-4
25	2 Samuel 17-18	Psalm 144	1 Thessalonians 5
26	2 Samuel 19	Psalm 145	2 Thessalonians 1-3
27	2 Samuel 20-21	Psalm 146	1 Timothy 1-2
28	2 Samuel 22	Psalm 147	1 Timothy 3-4
29	2 Samuel 23-24	Psalm 148	1 Timothy 5-6
30	1 Kings 1	Psalm 149	2 Timothy 1-2
31	1 Kings 2-3	Psalm 150	2 Timothy 3-4

June

1	1 Kings 4-5	Proverbs 1	Titus 1-3
2	1 Kings 6-7	Proverbs 2	Philemon
3	1 Kings 8	Proverbs 3	Hebrews 1-2
4	1 Kings 9-10	Proverbs 4	Hebrews 3-4
5	1 Kings 11-12	Proverbs 5	Hebrews 5-6
6	1 Kings 13-14	Proverbs 6	Hebrews 7-8
7	1 Kings 15-16	Proverbs 7	Hebrews 9-10
8	1 Kings 17-18	Proverbs 8	Hebrews 11
9	1 Kings 19-20	Proverbs 9	Hebrews 12
10	1 Kings 21-22	Proverbs 10	Hebrews 13
11	2 Kings 1-2	Proverbs 11	James 1
12	2 Kings 3-4	Proverbs 12	James 2-3
13	2 Kings 5-6	Proverbs 13	James 4-5
14	2 Kings 7-8	Proverbs 14	1 Peter 1
15	2 Kings 9-10	Proverbs 15	1 Peter 2-3
16	2 Kings 11-12	Proverbs 16	1 Peter 4-5
17	2 Kings 13-14	Proverbs 17	2 Peter 1-3
18	2 Kings 15-16	Proverbs 18	1 John 1-2
19	2 Kings 17	Proverbs 19	1 John 3-4
20	2 Kings 18-19	Proverbs 20	1 John 5
21	2 Kings 20-21	Proverbs 21	2 John
22	2 Kings 22-23	Proverbs 22	3 John
23	2 Kings 24-25	Proverbs 23	Jude
24	1 Chronicles 1	Proverbs 24	Revelation 1-2
25	1 Chronicles 2-3	Proverbs 25	Revelation 3-5
26	1 Chronicles 4-5	Proverbs 26	Revelation 6-7
27	1 Chronicles 6-7	Proverbs 27	Revelation 8-10
28	1 Chronicles 8-9	Proverbs 28	Revelation 11-12
29	1 Chronicles 10-11	Proverbs 29	Revelation 13-14
30	1 Chronicles 12-13	Proverbs 30	Revelation 15-17

July

1	1 Chronicles 14-15	Proverbs 31	Revelation 18-19
2	1 Chronicles 16-17	Psalm 1	Revelation 20-22
3	1 Chronicles 18-19	Psalm 2	Matthew 1-2
4	1 Chronicles 20-21	Psalm 3	Matthew 3-4
5	1 Chronicles 22-23	Psalm 4	Matthew 5
6	1 Chronicles 24-25	Psalm 5	Matthew 6-7
7	1 Chronicles 26-27	Psalm 6	Matthew 8-9
8	1 Chronicles 28-29	Psalm 7	Matthew 10-11
9	2 Chronicles 1-2	Psalm 8	Matthew 12
10	2 Chronicles 3-4	Psalm 9	Matthew 13
11	2 Chronicles 5-6	Psalm 10	Matthew 14-15
12	2 Chronicles 7-8	Psalm 11	Matthew 16-17
13	2 Chronicles 9-10	Psalm 12	Matthew 18
14	2 Chronicles 11-12	Psalm 13	Matthew 19-20
15	2 Chronicles 13-14	Psalm 14	Matthew 21
16	2 Chronicles 15-16	Psalm 15	Matthew 22
17	2 Chronicles 17-18	Psalm 16	Matthew 23
18	2 Chronicles 19-20	Psalm 17	Matthew 24
19	2 Chronicles 21-22	Psalm 18	Matthew 25
20	2 Chronicles 23-24	Psalm 19	Matthew 26
21	2 Chronicles 25-26	Psalm 20	Matthew 27
22	2 Chronicles 27-28	Psalm 21	Matthew 28
23	2 Chronicles 29-30	Psalm 22	Mark 1
24	2 Chronicles 31-32	Psalm 23	Mark 2
25	2 Chronicles 33-34	Psalm 24	Mark 3
26	2 Chronicles 35-36	Psalm 25	Mark 4
27	Ezra 1-2	Psalm 26	Mark 5
28	Ezra 3-4	Psalm 27	Mark 6
29	Ezra 5-6	Psalm 28	Mark 7
30	Ezra 7-8	Psalm 29	Mark 8
31	Ezra 9-10	Psalm 30	Mark 9

August

1	Nehemiah 1-2	Psalm 31	Mark 10
2	Nehemiah 3-4	Psalm 32	Mark 11
3	Nehemiah 5-6	Psalm 33	Mark 12
4	Nehemiah 7	Psalm 34	Mark 13
5	Nehemiah 8-9	Psalm 35	Mark 14
6	Nehemiah 10-11	Psalm 36	Mark 15
7	Nehemiah 12-13	Psalm 37	Mark 16
8	Esther 1-2	Psalm 38	Luke 1
9	Esther 3-4	Psalm 39	Luke 2
10	Esther 5-6	Psalm 40	Luke 3
11	Esther 7-8	Psalm 41	Luke 4
12	Esther 9-10	Psalm 42	Luke 5
13	Job 1-2	Psalm 43	Luke 6
14	Job 3-4	Psalm 44	Luke 7
15	Job 5-6	Psalm 45	Luke 8
16	Job 7-8	Psalm 46	Luke 9
17	Job 9-10	Psalm 47	Luke 10
18	Job 11-12	Psalm 48	Luke 11
19	Job 13-14	Psalm 49	Luke 12
20	Job 15-16	Psalm 50	Luke 13
21	Job 17-18	Psalm 51	Luke 14
22	Job 19-20	Psalm 52	Luke 15
23	Job 21-22	Psalm 53	Luke 16
24	Job 23-25	Psalm 54	Luke 17
25	Job 26-28	Psalm 55	Luke 18
26	Job 29-30	Psalm 56	Luke 19
27	Job 31-32	Psalm 57	Luke 20
28	Job 33-34	Psalm 58	Luke 21
29	Job 35-36	Psalm 59	Luke 22
30	Job 37-38	Psalm 60	Luke 23
31	Job 39-40	Psalm 61	Luke 24

September

1	Job 41-42	Psalm 62	John 1
2	Ecclesiastes 1-2	Psalm 63	John 2-3
3	Ecclesiastes 3-4	Psalm 64	John 4
4	Ecclesiastes 5-6	Psalm 65	John 5
5	Ecclesiastes 7-8	Psalm 66	John 6
6	Ecclesiastes 9-10	Psalm 67	John 7
7	Ecclesiastes 1-12	Psalm 68	John 8
8	Song of Solomon 1-2	Psalm 69	John 9
9	Song of Solomon 3-4	Psalm 70	John 10
10	Song of Solomon 5-6	Psalm 71	John 11
11	Song of Solomon 7-8	Psalm 72	John 12
12	Isaiah 1-2	Psalm 73	John 13
13	Isaiah 3-5	Psalm 74	John 14-15
14	Isaiah 6-8	Psalm 75	John 16
15	Isaiah 9-10	Psalm 76	John 17
16	Isaiah 11-13	Psalm 77	John 18
17	Isaiah 14-15	Psalm 78	John 19
18	Isaiah 16-17	Psalm 79	John 20
19	Isaiah 18-19	Psalm 80	John 21
20	Isaiah 20-22	Psalm 81	Acts 1
21	Isaiah 23-24	Psalm 82	Acts 2
22	Isaiah 25-26	Psalm 83	Acts 3-4
23	Isaiah 27-28	Psalm 84	Acts 5-6
24	Isaiah 29-30	Psalm 85	Acts 7
25	Isaiah 31-32	Psalm 86	Acts 8
26	Isaiah 33-34	Psalm 87	Acts 9
27	Isaiah 35-36	Psalm 88	Acts 10
28	Isaiah 37-38	Psalm 89	Acts 11-12
29	Isaiah 39-40	Psalm 90	Acts 13
30	Isaiah 41-42	Psalm 91	Acts 14

October

1	Isaiah 43-44	Psalm 92	Acts 15
2	Isaiah 45-46	Psalm 93	Acts 16
3	Isaiah 47-48	Psalm 94	Acts 17
4	Isaiah 49-50	Psalm 95	Acts 18
5	Isaiah 51-52	Psalm 96	Acts 19
6	Isaiah 53-54	Psalm 97	Acts 20
7	Isaiah 55-56	Psalm 98	Acts 21
8	Isaiah 57-58	Psalm 99	Acts 22
9	Isaiah 59-60	Psalm 100	Acts 23
10	Isaiah 61-62	Psalm 101	Acts 24-25
11	Isaiah 63-64	Psalm 102	Acts 26
12	Isaiah 65-66	Psalm 103	Acts 27
13	Jeremiah 1-2	Psalm 104	Acts 28
14	Jeremiah 3-4	Psalm 105	Romans 1-2
15	Jeremiah 5-6	Psalm 106	Romans 3-4
16	Jeremiah 7-8	Psalm 107	Romans 5-6
17	Jeremiah 9-10	Psalm 108	Romans 7-8
18	Jeremiah 11-12	Psalm 109	Romans 9-10
19	Jeremiah 13-14	Psalm 110	Romans 11-12
20	Jeremiah 15-16	Psalm 111	Romans 13-14
21	Jeremiah 17-18	Psalm 112	Romans 15-16
22	Jeremiah 19-20	Psalm 113	1 Corinthians 1-2
23	Jeremiah 21-22	Psalm 114	1 Corinthians 3-4
24	Jeremiah 23-24	Psalm 115	1 Corinthians 5-6
25	Jeremiah 25-26	Psalm 116	1 Corinthians 7
26	Jeremiah 27-28	Psalm 117	1 Corinthians 8-9
27	Jeremiah 29-30	Psalm 118	1 Corinthians 10
28	Jeremiah 31-32	Psalm 119: 1-64	1 Corinthians 11
29	Jeremiah 33-34	Psalm 119:65-120	1 Corinthians 12
30	Jeremiah 35-36	Psalm 119:121-176	1 Corinthians 13
31	Jeremiah 37-38	Psalm 120	1 Corinthians 14

November

1	Jeremiah 39-40	Psalm 121	1 Corinthians 15
2	Jeremiah 41-42	Psalm 122	1 Corinthians 16
3	Jeremiah 43-44	Psalm 123	2 Corinthians 1
4	Jeremiah 45-46	Psalm 124	2 Corinthians 2-3
5	Jeremiah 47-48	Psalm 125	2 Corinthians 4-5
6	Jeremiah 49-50	Psalm 126	2 Corinthians 6-7
7	Jeremiah 51-52	Psalm 127	2 Corinthians 8
8	Lamentations 1-2	Psalm 128	2 Corinthians 9-10
9	Lamentations 3	Psalm 129	2 Corinthians 11
10	Lamentations 4-5	Psalm 130	2 Corinthians 12
11	Ezekiel 1-2	Psalm 131	2 Corinthians 13
12	Ezekiel 3-4	Psalm 132	Galatians 1-2
13	Ezekiel 5-6	Psalm 133	Galatians 3-4
14	Ezekiel 7-8	Psalm 134	Galatians 5-6
15	Ezekiel 9-10	Psalm 135	Ephesians 1-2
16	Ezekiel 11-12	Psalm 136	Ephesians 3-4
17	Ezekiel 13-14	Psalm 137	Ephesians 5-6
18	Ezekiel 15-16	Psalm 138	Philippians 1-2
19	Ezekiel 17-18	Psalm 139	Philippians 3-4
20	Ezekiel 19-20	Psalm 140	Colossians 1-2
21	Ezekiel 21-22	Psalm 141	Colossians 3-4
22	Ezekiel 23-24	Psalm 142	1 Thessalonians 1-2
23	Ezekiel 25-26	Psalm 143	1 Thessalonians 3-4
24	Ezekiel 27-28	Psalm 144	1 Thessalonians 5
25	Ezekiel 29-30	Psalm 145	2 Thessalonians 1-3
26	Ezekiel 31-32	Psalm 146	1 Timothy 1-2
27	Ezekiel 33-34	Psalm 147	1 Timothy 3-4
28	Ezekiel 35-36	Psalm 148	1 Timothy 5-6
29	Ezekiel 37-38	Psalm 149	2 Timothy 1-2
30	Ezekiel 39-40	Psalm 150	2 Timothy 3-4

December

1	Ezekiel 41-42	Proverbs 1	Titus 1-3
2	Ezekiel 43-44	Proverbs 2	Philemon
3	Ezekiel 45-46	Proverbs 3	Hebrews 1-2
4	Ezekiel 47-48	Proverbs 4	Hebrews 3-4
5	Daniel 1-2	Proverbs 5	Hebrews 5-6
6	Daniel 3-4	Proverbs 6	Hebrews 7-8
7	Daniel 5-6	Proverbs 7	Hebrews 9-10
8	Daniel 7-8	Proverbs 8	Hebrews 11
9	Daniel 9-10	Proverbs 9	Hebrews 12
10	Daniel 11-12	Proverbs 10	Hebrews 13
11	Hosea 1-3	Proverbs 11	James 1-3
12	Hosea 4-6	Proverbs 12	James 4-5
13	Hosea 7-8	Proverbs 13	1 Peter 1
14	Hosea 9-11	Proverbs 14	1 Peter 2-3
15	Hosea 12-14	Proverbs 15	1 Peter 4-5
16	Joel 1-3	Proverbs 16	2 Peter 1-3
17	Amos 1-3	Proverbs 17	1 John 1-2
18	Amos 4-6	Proverbs 18	1 John 3-4
19	Amos 7-9	Proverbs 19	1 John 5
20	Obadiah	Proverbs 20	2 John
21	Jonah 1-4	Proverbs 21	3 John
22	Micah 1-4	Proverbs 22	Jude
23	Micah 5-7	Proverbs 23	Revelation 1-2
24	Nahum 1-3	Proverbs 24	Revelation 3-5
25	Habakkuk 1-3	Proverbs 25	Revelation 6-7
26	Zephaniah 1-3	Proverbs 26	Revelation 8-10
27	Haggai 1-2	Proverbs 27	Revelation 11-12
28	Zechariah 1-4	Proverbs 28	Revelation 13-14
29	Zechariah 5-9	Proverbs 29	Revelation 15-17
30	Zechariah 10-14	Proverbs 30	Revelation 18-19
31	Malachi 1-4	Proverbs 31	Revelation 20-22